Experiencing The Lovers Dialog Between Church, World and God: in the pastoral prayer

by
J. Kent Borgaard

Bloomington, IN   Milton Keynes, UK

authorHOUSE®

AuthorHouse™
1663 Liberty Drive, Suite 200
Bloomington, IN 47403
www.authorhouse.com
Phone: 1-800-839-8640

AuthorHouse™ UK Ltd.
500 Avebury Boulevard
Central Milton Keynes, MK9 2BE
www.authorhouse.co.uk
Phone: 08001974150

First published by AuthorHouse 1/8/2007

ISBN: 978-1-4259-6546-4 (sc)

Printed in the United States of America
Bloomington, Indiana

This book is printed on acid-free paper.

Discovering together
An unexpected intimacy
Initiated by a "Yearning God"

DEDICATION

My wife, Mary, and I, along with my mother in her early 90's during her final illness, were remembering our way through a lifetime of family accumulations ... reminders of some of the building materials used by our Creator in the never ending process of our ongoing creation.

There in one of Mom's scrapbooks was a newspaper copy of the prayer my Army Chaplain father, Captain Raymond D. Borgaard, had been asked to lead at Fort Warren, Wyoming during a celebration ceremony at the ending of WW II. What a meaningful task and privilege this had been for him, as he reflected upon the deadly serious ministry he had provided to that now almost unimaginable horde of our youth; who had simply gulped down a deep breath, and stepped up to take on the most humanly impossible task in the history of the world. His attempt to serve their needs had remained the absolute highlight of his life.

Over one another's shoulders we had read through this prayer together and remained quiet for a few moments ... until Mary broke the silence:

"Why; that sounds just like you!"

Until that moment I don't think I had ever even begun to realize just how much we have all been put together by our Creator ... using all of the materials around us ... for good or ill.

We rub off on one another!

Both Dad and I are bundles of contradictions. We illustrate the "rubbing off on one another" as a part of such a process of creation, and I felt good about what Mary had just exclaimed.

Proof reading through this book before publication, I cannot avoid seeing paraded in its pages parts of my bundle of contradictions, and realizing how very grateful I am for the gift of vulnerable humanness which they illustrate. How wise and trusting of our Creator to have incorporated every bit of it into the process ... so ...

Dad,
it's all dedicated to you.
How I wish I could communicate
to my world,
in the way you were able to speak
through word and deed,
to the pressing needs of that
"Greatest Generation" of all,

- - - - - - - - - - -

as Tom Brokaw has so aptly named them in retrospect.

i hope you approve

TABLE OF CONTENTS

BEFORE-WORD

On a good Sabbath, as the pastoral prayer draws to a close the congregation returns to earth knowing itself to really *be* the "Body of Christ" in ways which probably no one could ever explain, but which in this moment are known in the bones as well as the soul. Second only to its moments of sharing together the elements of Communion (The Lord's Supper, the Eucharist, the Mass, whatever it may be called in a specific church's tradition), this is the moment when a congregation may rise to just such a level of knowing beyond believing. Now it knows it lives for a reason, and that reason is to actively enter into the life and being of all that is ... that, indeed, "in him (Christ) all things (really do) hold together!" (Col 1:17) At its best, the Pastoral Prayer may result in something like that.

But you don't need anyone to tell you that it isn't always that way, do you? That highly potential moment may come and go ... and very little, really, has happened. Consider some of the ways in which the Pastoral Prayer is allowed to become so much less than its potential:

- Without full consciousness of what is happening, one leader of the prayer may carefully explain to God why we are gathered together, while the worshipers wonder under their breath if the Creator did not, maybe, already know.

- Another may express the desires of the congregation in such a way that they sound like direct (do this, do that) instructions as to how God should respond. Had the Creator failed to notice the need? Or might the Creator yearn for our response, rather than our "directions?"

- Another may be so caught up in the "order and sequence of items to be included," as learned in seminary or in workshops on prayer, that it all becomes more nearly an exercise in proper liturgy than a communication of immediate personal or corporate or of-the-universe relationships and concerns.

- Yet another may be so caught up in the needs of a world gone astray that the support-and-celebration needs of the congregation and its members are totally forgotten; or, on the other hand, may dwell so much on the aches and pains and trophies of the members that the world out there never ever penetrates the walls of the sanctuary.

- You've certainly been distracted by hearing prayers so obviously "composed" in some ivory tower that they just can't be "spoken" as conversation. And you've no doubt heard others, obviously not written, but so "jargonistic" that, if you move in the same circles, you may be able to finish the sentences before the leader of the prayer gets there.

What pastor, attempting to be worthy of the title, has not listened in upon a tape of the service and exclaimed (something like) "Oh no! I didn't say that … did I?"… or," It wasn't supposed to sound like that!" Some unplanned and unseen filter seems to have slipped in and changed things. What might have been a live sharing with the congregation of one struggler's wrestling of the soul with the Creator in light of the current situation has become part of a stereotyped "program" designed to some kind of lowest common denominator. A transformer has entered into the circuit and stepped 220 volts of alternating current down to 6 volts of "direct" one way trickle. The result may have fit in with the planning of the moment but fails to facilitate any kind of engagement with the yearned-for and promised "***Presence***"… "*wherever two or more are gathered in my name.*"

CRITIQUING TOWARD THE FUTURE

As a pastoral care person who has wrestled with such concerns for 24 years as a Parish Pastor, then Director of Pastoral Care at a 340 bed General Hospital[1]; then Pastoral Services Coordinator at a Psychiatric and Community Mental Health Complex[2]; the Pastoral Prayer question has been a constant and haunting presence. During the non congregationally-related ministries there was the added complication of operating in an environment where there was no congregation to provide history and context, as during a hospital chapel service … or where you were a relative stranger to the congregational context, as when filling a pulpit where you were not "the pastor"…or when you have been asked to put in an eternal context some community event or meal where you sense that some don't even feel you should be there; but you just know the occasion really does call for and would be enhanced by a genuine pastoral touch … which just might serve as an invitation for some of those present to sense their activity to be a form of dialog with the Creator, even though it may be happening in a secular setting.

So the question never goes away: How can the pastoral prayer be put together to more consistently engage both presenter and hearers, yet with the filters left out, and enough chinks and cracks left in so that this elusive

---

[1] Elkhart General Hospital, Elkhart, IN

[2] Oaklawn Psychiatric and Community Health Complex (affiliated with the Mennonite Church, and Church of the Brethren), Elkhart County, IN

haunting "Presence" might more often slip in through our offered-up imperfections and once more transform our yearnings and doubts and hopes and fears and joys into a shared experience of eternity in time? How can such moments be presented as opportunities to lay our humanness in those eternal hands with the expectation that there all things will, indeed, prove to hold together with that which is eternal … as promised.

How indeed?!

At this point memories of dealing with supervision and accountability, and reporting and record keeping in the institutional setting began to bring to mind words such as "critique:" Look *critically* at what has been happening in order to gain perspective for the future. Ponder both the strengths and the weaknesses: How has the activity fulfilled or not fulfilled its purpose? Look back and ahead in the same moment, so that what has been may contribute constructively to what is yet to be.

So the intention here is to critique … to pull up and record attempts of pastoral prayers in a variety of contexts, from the past and the present and projected toward the future, and to look at them with an eye to what might have been or what might yet be. Perhaps a second look may help us to grow in our sense of corporate experience of "the Presence." The original intent was to help me, personally, in my own pilgrimage. But if these pages can be a source of help in the pilgrimage of others with whom they might be shared, that will be a very personally satisfying bonus.

Ideally, my hope would be that reading through this process might trigger in the reader an impulse towards developing an ongoing practice of retrieving his or her own pastoral prayer offerings and developing some kind of continuing critique for the purpose of enhancing the corporate worship of the congregation. Surely this would also enhance the pastor's contacts and communications with other corporate groups in the community served by the congregation which she or he represents. And, for the lay reader, insight into dialog with the pastoral leadership about the continually evolving forms of ministry to its members and to the world just might be enhanced as well.

THE RAW MATERIAL

Some of the materials included here are taken from the manuscripts of prayers prepared for specific occasions. Some are attempts to remember and retrieve non-manuscripted prayers. Many will be combinations of the above, for seldom is it possible for me to get through a prepared prayer without on-the-spot ad-lib alterations in response to the continual promptings "of the Spirit." Some will be current in-the-mill anticipations of pending corporate prayer occasions. (As a person who has seldom managed to rise above a rather undisciplined personal prayer life, these latter have proven to be one way of incarnating the flow of inner promptings. If not brought to the light of day and given flesh, bone and heart … through the medium of pen and paper, or word processor, or verbal sharing with another person …such inner nudges often simply fritter away and are forever lost to consciousness).

The original corpus of prayer material comes from the 1990's while I was primarily on the staff of the Psychiatric Complex, but also serving part-time on the staff of First Christian Church (Disciples of Christ) in South Bend, Indiana … before gradually retiring by stages. Added to this material for Reflection (critique) are other materials from various ministries in the more distant past, and present special assignment ministries. Sprinkled through it all will be some prayers used on interdenominational or secular occasions, where … however they might have seen it … I knew it to be pastoral in intent. If not, why would they have invited a pastor to take on the task?

Where the text of the prayer may refer to specific historically newsworthy events (such as "Kosovo"), there was always the temptation to simply substitute the name of a more recent similar happening, and this has made me so very aware of the fact that such things are always with us. However in most cases I have opted to leave it the way it was; at least partly to appeal to the power of nostalgia in the case of any readers who may remember the event, and capitalize on the "anchoring" value of being able to relate to a personal "been there … done that" memory.

As the purpose is to critique the original material, I have tried to resist the temptation to clean it up too much in terms of sentence structure, punctuation and the like. For it to sound as much like it might have sounded then, _it will be important for the reader to "speak" it internally, rather than just read it_. The division indication of three dots … will often be used to indicate a related thought that is much like a new sentence … but not quite. Like the communications of the Apostle Paul … which often come across as interminably long sentences … but which require connections between his related thoughts …which would be disturbed by a multitude of separate sentences … so if you kept tracing back to each antecedent thought you would eventually find yourself at the starting point: "Paul, an apostle of Jesus Christ . . . . . . "If that seems like trying to justify my undisciplined styles of prayer, and of writing, by invoking the presence of the Apostle Paul … so be it. One could do worse.

A THEOLOGICAL PERSPECTIVE

for Praying the Pastoral Prayer
as Lovers Dialog between Church, World, and God

Of course it is important that a conscious Biblical/Theological perspective undergird anything as important as the central prayer each week, when the congregation in which our faith is nurtured gathers for worship and we experience our "one-another-ness" under God. For on this experience is founded our growth in Christ, and here we receive and hone the tools for ministry in and to the world. So let us consider at least one such perspective.

Marriage as a Biblical Metaphor

It is certainly no accident that the Bible turns again and again to the metaphor of marriage, as it struggles to speak of the committed relationship between God and God's people. And what a powerful image that is! For, try as we might, no one has ever been able to explain or adequately describe the kind of give-and-take which goes into the relationship between wife and husband which gives it the potential for the deepest possible intimacy and blessing, surpassing all other relationships this side of the Divine. The full bliss of *receiving* the love of the other can never be fully known unless the receiver is unreservedly *giving* at the same moment in the dance of committed relationship. It is a dialog of deeply and profoundly listening and speaking, touching and being touched, in the same moment. And as tongue-tied mortals try to describe the process, often they end up stammering out words to the effect that their experience of giving and receiving from the essence of one another, in all of their (so profound) differences and oppositions, somehow seems to be a bridge between body and spirit, heaven and earth, time and eternity.

Those differences hold together in a mysterious, wondrous *creativity*. No wonder the Bible, in its impossible concern to describe the indescribable, has picked up and leaned upon this metaphor as it tries to draw us further into creative relationship between one-another, God, and all those born into "the image" of God. Into the *Mystery!*

So we find the Old Testament prophets describing a covenant relationship between God and Israel, in which each yearns for fulfillment together in relationship with the other, and their metaphor is that of husband and wife.

"Prophets found in the mutuality of attraction and obligations, which most of them experienced in marriage, the symbol of a lasting relationship. For them the covenant between Yahweh and Israel was like a marriage across the centuries. They used the imagery of marital love as a figure of religious behavior enduring in time.

> 'As the bridegroom rejoices over the bride,
> So shall your God rejoice over you.'" (Isa 62:5)[3]

And the New Testament continues to speak of the church (the Christian extension and/or equivalent of Israel) as the Body of Christ, made ready for the marriage of the Lamb (Rev 19:7) with the ultimate fulfillment compared to the celebration of a marriage feast.

Deepen Or Die

One of the basic discoveries of those attempting to live (and possibly beginning to discover the very meaning of their lives) in this kind of divine/human intimacy, is the mutual realization that the relationship continues to deepen …or it begins to die. For never, ever, is it complete, and, therefore, static. Always something more can be sensed, rooted in and emerging from what has already been in the relationship. So the quiet highlight for many such lovers has been that moment, as the dark of evening begins to put all of creation in perspective, when each relates to the other their part of the day's journey, experienced while they were apart … when each brings and presents their other-ness to the one-another-ness of the relationship. And it is from the intimacy of this meeting that *whatever* will be born next from the relationship is conceived and begins the gestation process of coming into being. Partners in Creation!

Celebrating Creation

In the intimacy of such moments of coming together in "conception dialog," either one or both of the partners may sometimes experience the quiet tears … which Carl Rogers has described as a sign of the moment when a person either hears the indescribable depths behind what is being related by the other, or realizes that the other has heard those indescribable depths in him or her self. Some couples experience such moments as a bridge between time and eternity. And this may well be a part of the prelude to further joyous body/spirit (read: time/eternity) celebration of the growing, 24 hours a day, body/spirit, intimacy between them.

On Earth As It Is In Heaven

"Our Father, who art in heaven, hallowed be thy name. Thy kingdom come, thy will be done, on earth as it is in heaven." There it is!: Modeled for us by Jesus, himself … the heart of all genuine prayer dialog. There it is

---

[3] Samuel Terrien, *"TILL THE HEART SINGS, A Biblical Theology of Manhood and Womanhood,* Philadelphia, Fortress Press, 1985, Pp 52-53

...that bridge between heaven and earth as the center of and the reason for our prayers. That it may be "... on earth as it is in heaven ..."

But how often do the ears of our hearts hear in that prayer-phrase, "on earth as it is in heaven," the perspective of a *yearning* God, just waiting for those created in the image of God to really seriously open their hearts to the Lover/Creator's entering in (that God may have an invited-into place in the experience of earth) ... never forcing, just waiting like a young lover walking alongside in hope that the other person will brush hands as a tentative invitation for hands, then, to be tenderly joined in expression of a growing relationship. The human (earth) side now responding to the divine touch ...saying, "Look, I am no longer asking, please do this-or-that for me," but instead, saying, "See, I am as open as I can be for you to enter in ...that earth (me) and heaven (you) may know the touch of living relationship, whatever may happen. (Moving both ways.)

For so many the tendency has been to think most often of prayer as simply petition--asking for the meeting of perceived needs. Seldom do we hear God speaking as the Old Testament prophet, Hosea, heard:

"When Israel was a child, I loved *him*, and out of Egypt I called *my child*. The more I called *them* the more they went from me ... yet it was I who taught (*them*) to walk, I took them up in my arms; but they did not know that I healed them. I led them with cords of human kindness, with bands of love. I was to them like those who lift infants to their cheeks. I bent down to them and fed them . . . . How can I give you up . . . . How can I hand you over . . . .My heart recoils within me; my compassion grows warm and tender." (Hosea 11:1-4, 8)

Of course *this is metaphorical.* And, remember, it grew out of Hosea's frustrated lover's relationship with the unfaithful Gomer. But it was what Hosea, through the experience of seeking her out in her straying, buying her back from slavery and forgiving her *as she was*, heard God speaking. And how can we ever hear those words in such a context and miss that plaintive sense of, "Won't they ever respond and let me in so we may be in lover's dialog? so that we can communicate ourselves to one another in loving/intimate relationship . . . . . . ?"

. . . So that it can be . . .on earth as it is in heaven . . . . ?"

Is this what Hosea heard his Creator saying ... that the need is not only ours for God, but also God's need to be freely and passionately invited into our earthly lives?; as Hosea yearned to be freely invited *back into the life of the unfaithful Gomer? That the God/human relationship in creation can never be complete until there has also been such a matching human initiative? It sounds that way, doesn't it? And it certainly is Biblical!*

The "Pillow-Talk" Portion of the Sunday Morning Liturgy

So it is … that after the successes and failures of the week the congregation returns to the setting of their most intimate earth/heaven relationship experiences … (much as the couple returns to the "safe" setting of their one-another-ness after the successes and failures of the day). Here it is all put into perspective through the intimacy of open dialog between the individuals, the congregation, and their God. *Here the relationship is up front.* Here the successes are celebrated together and comfort is shared for the failures. Thanks are given for the faithfulness, and forgiveness held out and received for any unfaithfulness that may have slipped into the equation. Here frustration may be expressed (and lovingly heard) of our inability to understand and our deficiencies in loving. *And here, in the recognition, and acceptance, and celebration of it all, the seeds are sown which may germinate as we begin to look forward with anticipation towards the emergence (birth … or born-again-ness) of that which can always be counted upon to grow out of the fertilization of each intimate encounter.*[4]

The Pastor As FACILITATOR

And if the congregation has been taught to understand the pastoral prayer as this kind of dialog, then the pastor becomes, not the "congregation's designated pray-er" (*for* them), but the *facilitator* of *the congregation's* dialog with their passionate, Lover/God, who yearns to be genuinely invited in. As the pastor begins to function in this role, the direction and the style begins to change. It becomes much more intimately conversational in its expression. Openness to listening, questioning, brief moments of silence as in any living dialog, become more natural and spontaneous. Simple petitions for forgiveness begin to lead to the discovery of the depth of the blindness or unfaithfulness behind the experience … and to immediate gratitude for the growing realization that any pain experienced by the forgiver may be balanced out by the joy of having been invited into the relationship by the simple, trusting act of asking for the forgiveness.

---

[4] Though some may be able to think only in terms of heterosexual marriage; might not the metaphor for others include the yearning and responsiveness experienced in the intimacy of genuinely committed, same sex unions? … as each discovers and draws from the other the feminine and masculine components that mingle together in every human personality. I only ask.

Then, in congregations where the worship will be finally summed up in the celebration of Communion, Eucharist, Lord's Supper, Mass … whatever it be called in their particular tradition … the summing-up, sealing, culminating earth/heaven experience will take place under the umbrella of those instituting words, "This is my *body* … my *life blood* … given to and for you." ***Lover's-dialog-language***!

In traditions where this is not a weekly occurrence, it must be assumed that the facilitating pastor will continue to hold before the congregation the memory and the centrality of that gratefully shared Eucharist meal, so that the "heart" of the divine/earthy, body-and-blood connection will be ever in their experience of thanksgiving prayer together "*as the Body*." And their praying may begin to grow into so much more of a body/spirit connection … "On earth as it is in heaven."

So … Let Us Critique Away . . . .

AN INVITATION TO FLOW WITH THE FORMAT

The original intention for this presentation was that each prayer would fill
one page

And the opposing page would include equal space:
for reflection upon the prayer
by the author
and reflection upon the prayer
by the reader

HOWEVER
(always there seems to crop up a "however")

However … the necessity of moving to a smaller format
caused that fit not to fit …
so
in some cases, by giving up spaces between paragraphs
this may be possible … but not always
you'll see what we mean

And you are <u>invited</u> to scribble delightfully in the margins
and do whatever you must for your part of the intended dialog
and <u>expected</u> to forgive the writer for any long-windedness
and
Once in a while there may even be thrown in a whole
blank page or more for your own long winded exposition
How about <u>that</u> ? !

Please note, also, the email address of the author
kmborg1@aol.com
is intended to be taken seriously
for dialog

Wondrous Dialog
which just might raise the dead to new life

Talk to me!
But … of course … that is up to you

INCLUSION

God of our lives … God of every part of our lives … we thank and praise you for those alternations of Winter, Spring, Summer and Autumn … night and day … sunshine and rain … planting, growth and harvest … birth and death and all of the ages in between from childhood through adulthood. We thank and praise you for the rhythms of our existence by which we experience growth and variety and change in the midst of the consistency of this wondrous universe into which you have birthed us as our home.

Forgive us when we begin to take it all for granted and cease to notice. Forgive us when we begin to claim it, each person and group of persons for their own, as if it were not to be rightly shared and enjoyed and preserved together by all whom you have called into being. Forgive us for so often pulling away and making orphans of ourselves when you have given us so much family. Forgive us for failing to notice as you continually parent us through it all, so that our hearing and sight grow dim to the many quiet, non-coercive ways you still reach out to woo us and nudge us towards one another, and, thus, draw us to yourself.

O God, in Christ we experience the complete, fulfilled, human response to it all, and hear the human plea that we commit ourselves, and return your love by our caring for those others with whom you have chosen to enfold us in the bundle of life. So we assume it must be very "right" when we ache and agonize for those who find themselves hunted down or killed or driven out by others who you intended to be sisters and brothers. Forgive us when we cease to hurt for, or even look towards, the many open sores upon the skin of your good Earth.

And grant us open eyes and hearts as we pause in these moments to focus on those close by, of our own number, who struggle with burdens beyond their understanding, or who would invite us into their struggles. Let none of those among us feel as orphans when you have promised us the constancy of your love, and called us to be the family through which it is known. We pray in the name and spirit of Jesus Christ.   Amen

Reflections

What about those in the congregation who really do not sense themselves to be a part of it all; who may possibly be blocked by past experiences so they cannot yet understand this as context; for whom the experience of "orphan" may still be the most real, and seemingly inescapable part of their lives? Perhaps it is justified to keep putting this before them and attempting to draw them into it, but might it not have felt more inclusive to them had mention been made that there is such a category of experiencers who feel <u>ex</u>clusion because of the inability in these moments to feel their <u>in</u>clusion; that to be in this category is not a sin, but a part of the "wilderness experience" which is a part of <u>everyone's</u> life at different stages?

I wish I had done this. It might have helped them to feel included, and pointed towards those dark moments when even the rest of us feel lost and must simply rest in trust upon a grace which accepts us as we are, and enfolds us as we await a return to the holding together of all things. But, how would you say that?

Reader Reflections

JUST AS WE ARE

We praise you, God, for the amazing promise that your love comes to us just as we are. We praise you for the promise, but we must confess that we will probably never, ever, get it into our heads how this can be. In a world where time-cards are carefully tended to determine the pay we receive; where pensions are meted out according to the number of years employed; where a beautiful face and figure is really the first requirement for becoming Miss America, and those blessed with the rippling muscles, coordination and stamina to compete in the sports world receive tuition grants and multi-million dollar contracts, while many a caring dedicated, hard-working Nurse's Aid gives up in despair of ever earning even a subsistence wage, let alone enough to love and raise a family … in a world such as this it is a mind-blower to be able to sing, "Just as I am, thou wilt receive," and to … somehow … begin to believe it. We will probably never, ever, get into our <u>heads</u> how this can be … so we pray this morning that maybe we might, somehow, get it into our <u>hearts</u>.

Can it really be true that we can turn to you after all the unkind, unloving, unfaithful things we have done over a lifetime, and be loved as much as Mother Teresa is loved? Not in our heads it can't; in our hearts let it be. Can it be that you call us to forgive those who have been the most unloving, because that is the way you continually forgive us? In our heads, probably "No;" but in our hearts … oh, let it be! Much as human lovers may be blind to the faults of the beloved … but maybe even more with you to us … oh, let it be!

So, now Jewish "children of Isaac" and Arab "children of Ishmael" seem, finally, to be working at least half-heartedly on tiny little steps toward one another. We pray they may graduate from saying in their heads, "We've got to protect our interests and maybe this is the only way," to saying with their hearts, "Enough, all ready; we are not only of the same species, but of the same family, so the interests of one must be the interests of all." As this begins to swell against the ancient tide, may the prayers of our hearts help that swell become a world-wide chorus of "reconciliation." Help us, we pray, to continue to grow until we know in our hearts that we are all of the same <u>family</u> … so when one hurts everyone hurts, when one celebrates everyone celebrates.

No, it doesn't seem to be natural … certainly not "head natural." But what goes on between lovers is never "head natural," is it? Perhaps we can begin to discover that such love has its source in your love of us … then perhaps we may also begin to wrap that love around our love and concern for our close-by sisters and brothers, such as:

10

Then … if we wrap that kind of spirit around our love and concern for those members of our closer, more immediate family, could it be that we might at least begin to wrap it a-round those who seem so much further away? So whatever else may come to those who hurt, or are estranged, may our prayers (and the actions growing from our prayers) help them begin to hear a louder and clearer refrain of "Just as we are, we will receive, for we are all in the family." In the spirit of the One who calls us all to be One … "Just as we are." Amen.

Reflections

All right, all right, a sermon has once again slipped into the prayer. I've got to be more on guard against that. But then … might the "sermon" be heard when the heart is opened out in prayer, in ways that it might not be heard in other kinds of discourse? And if so, is this a legitimate enough reason to blur those distinctions a bit? Looking back I now note that there seems to be an under-the-surface suggestion that, whether or not we are in a position to take immediate, personal physical action on world matters, our prayerful concentration may well still help to "swell" the needed tide. Maybe that could or should have been made more explicit. Maybe not. I see I am going to have to work on that question as I go through this critiquing process. Probably it's about time.

Reader Reflections

PAINS SHARED

O God, what a sobering month this has been! Help us … help us, we pray, to be somehow able to see it all through your eyes and … with your help … to respond to it all as you would respond. Do you suppose that is possible? If so, what a wonderful gift that would be … your gift to each of us (each one of us, and to us together as your people) …what a wonder - full gift to the world that would be. No. We realize we aren't big enough to really respond as you respond, but help us, at least … to try … to begin.

So "flight 800" now joins "Lokerbee" and becomes a part of the vocabulary of history, and with it we sense ourselves as a part of a world wanting to reach out and put our arms around those hundreds of grieving people who keep asking, "Why? Oh, Why?" … So the summer Olympics continue, with the celebration of our common humanity which the Olympics at its best is meant to stress and express, now overlaid with a kind of grim determination: "We will go on … so as not to be overcome by this creeping insanity which seems to lurk in every shadow." And, if we are honest, there is probably a dark corner in most of us which says, "When we find 'em, KILL 'EM; even that's too good for those who would try to indescrimately blow up a crowd of spectators."

But, wait a minute … we just asked to see it through your eyes, didn't we? Through the eyes of a divine parent, through eyes and a heart possibly asking, "How could my children have come to this? … How could they have allowed to grow a society where <u>anyone</u> could feel so alienated as to not want to be one of the brothers and sisters of the family into which I have birthed them and invited them to live? How could it be that any one of my children could express the apparent hopelessness of their life by an act which shouts out, 'A pox on all of you! I don't even want to be a part of you; I want to hurt you … '(as I have been hurt ? ? ?)

O God, forgive us for any part that any of us may have in growing a world where anyone could feel so alienated as this. Forgive us our part in the hurt at the very center of … apparently … so many lives … in the world you have given and "so loved." Thank you for risking to us that great gift of freedom to choose. Yet how it must pain you to see what we have done with such a great gift.

Then, help us to begin right close to home. Help us to reach out to any around us who hurt, who may need your forgiveness … (but maybe could recognize it only when held out by a human hand) … lest they begin to fall into the ranks of the alienated, lost-ones. Help us to remove, we pray, the vindictiveness that lurks within us, and replace it with the tender-heartedness of family members to every human who lives … that our lives may be lived as this prayer is being prayed … in the name and the Spirit of Jesus Christ. Amen.

Reflections

Woops! Here arises again a constant fear: Have I tried again to sneak a sermon into what was meant to be a prayer? I don't honestly know, but at the moment, feel prayer and teaching/learning/exhortation are so related that this approach may have been justified. There were plenty of intelligent people in the congregation, one of them a very competent psychiatrist. It would be hard for such persons to miss the public display of my own shadow side in the KILL 'EM interjection. (I wonder how the inflection came through?) Some may criticize me for projecting and displaying my own weaknesses and foibles so freely … but I will continue to steadfastly resist any attempt to set the pastor aside as a model of perfection to have the congregation's faith for them, rather than to be among them as a fellow cracked clay pot … as Paul has observed us all to be. So, on that front, as I think about it now, "Here I stand." Also, one of my pet criticisms of prayer is our tendency to give God orders. Do I seem to be doing that here? If so, how else could it be said? The "we pray" before any expression of need or desire helps, but doesn't wholly cover it. Anyway, here may be an example of the everyday necessity of choosing the lesser of two evils … and wondering if we have chosen right; or wrong. Yes, there are problems with these things, but still the prayers need to be prayed, and I have yet to work out a better way. I pray God understands.

Reader Reflections

EVENINGS ARE FOR PERSPECTIVE

Before the Dinner Meeting, beginning the interdenominational Annual Parish Resource Center Forum with Loren Mead at the Notre Dame Continuing Education Center 9/15/98

Introduction:

Here in the midst of a typically mad-press-of-time week (at least for many of us), I invite you to use these moments to begin to let go of it all, to allow yourself to consciously begin to breathe easily and feel the tension start to fall away ////// so, slow and deepen your breathing while I invite you to close your eyes and see if you can picture a scene with me: We are standing on the flight-deck of an aircraft carrier anchored in Manila Bay during the insanity of the Korean conflict. It is not so long after WW II and in the daylight could be seen the ugly, rusting, ruined hulks of naval craft destroyed during those previous moments of insanity. But now ... it is evening, and in the fading of the light (a part of God's great gift of evening), even such a scene as this begins to be pulled together into a vision of peace and hope beyond confusion. Can you picture and feel the peace in this scene? ///// Peace in the midst of the world ... as it is ... when evening has come?

Now ... so that we may truly participate <u>together</u> in these moments of prayer ... I invite all who are familiar with the words and melody to join me in a prayer we can all do together as you begin to recognize it here ... in the peace and quiet of this Michiana evening; please sing along:

The Prayer:

Fairest Lord, Jesus! Ruler of all nature! O thou of God, and man the Son! Thee will I cherish, Thee will I honor. Thou, my soul's glory, joy and crown! / / / / / / / / / / /

Thank you, God, for the peace of these moments in this gathered part of the community of the One we claim as the Lord of our lives. Thank you for the cycles of your creation which includes evening moments in which the rubble of our waywardness during the light of day may begin to be transformed and become a part of the good news of your forgiving love. Thank you for the way the melodies of that love sneak into our innermost being to speak what mere words alone could never say. So we pray now, not for your promised presence in this evening and tomorrow, but we do pray for open eyes and hearts that we may be attuned and aware of what you are doing in our midst. Thank you for celebration times of breaking bread together ... especially in the midst of the wondrous diversity we see around us ... as, through the delights of food, the abundance of the universe enters into our bodies and becomes a part of who we are … just as the melodies shared and the insights anticipated may become a part of the continuing creation of our very beings. May contrition, Ah-Ha! Moments … and hearty celebrative laughter at our human foibles, blend together as we give ourselves over now in the peace of evening to whatever eye-opening beginnings you have in store for us now … and in the new day tomorrow. In the name and spirit of Jesus, the Christ, our Lord. Amen

Reflections

So often really alive prayer may be energized by kinds of imagery that pull us "into the picture" and allow us through inner sight to experience depths which words may never plumb. But looking back on this and similar occasions I sometimes wonder how fair it is to push others in the directions of one's own imagery, when it could well short-circuit the pictures which might arise from their own depths. I think that ordinarily this is a fair and legitimate way of enabling corporate prayer, and will probably continue to do it, but I know I must be continually sensitive never to dictate, but to only suggest and invite. And my sense at the time was that our gentle singing together had opened the door for considerably more freedom in the forms of prayer. (But it wouldn't have had to be a hymn; right now I am remembering us on the same occasion two or three years earlier, singing the old camp and conference song, "Tell Me Why," and having people remark that they had almost forgotten it, but that it had triggered memories and made the prayer which followed so much more meaningful to them. (Is that good, or just schmaltzy? I'm still working on that …Could it be that sometimes schmaltzy might be good. You may wrestle with that.)

Sometimes, it seems to me, that such introductions to prayer catch people's attention and bring them into the experience in ways that might, otherwise, have passed them by.

Reader Reflections

SMALL STEPS ... BIG STEPS

Oh God, you who call us to find the meaning of our lives in that One-Another-ness which we discover in the Community of Christ, we lift up our hearts together in wonder and praise for that which we could never, ever, explain ... but which continues to put it all together: like the ground base of the organ intermingling with the pastoral piping of the flutes and the call to action of the trumpets ... all in one great harmonious masterpiece of comfort, call to action, and the promise of eternity, all rolled into one. Forgive us, God, where we do not understand, and sometimes miss the in-the-now fulfillment of the eternal promise. Yes, we miss it when it is right before us. We miss it by our grasping and clinging to the little bits and pieces (our own bits and pieces) of what you seem to have intended to be a mosaic masterpiece of wholeness ... where everyone and every thing comes to completeness through its relationship to everything else. Forgive us, for it seems simply too grand to be grasped amidst the limitations of our grasping humanness. Forgive us.

But, God, it would help so much if we could, somehow, sense that you notice and honor the small steps we do take towards being responsive to your "lovers call" to us. Could it be that, as parents rejoice over and beam at those first steps and mamma/dadda words ... could it be that you do celebrate these early steps with us? Most of us have had our own private, maybe tentative moments of prayer ... of wondering in the starry nights ... of reaching out to another ... not because the receiver of our reaching out was lovely, but because of his or her own need.

And, in that, we are here, finding a special meaning we cannot explain as we allow you to enfold us in the one-another-ness of worship and prayer together. As we share in the bread and the cup we may begin to sense the mystery of that one body into which we are called. And as we begin that seemingly mundane task of gathering up and committing the first portion of our time, talents and wealth toward the insurance, health and vitality for this part of the "body of Christ" ... well, surely it must say something about our response to your call to "be here" for those who turn to you through this congregation...and for the world which you have "so loved." So we lift our prayers for

... may it possibly even bring tears to our eyes as we sense the won-der of the way you take the one and the one and the lonely one of us, and the fearful one of us, and the struggling one of us, and the loving one of us, into a warm one-another-ness of us as we respond (whether it is in small, creeping steps or gigantic strides) to the love you have extended through Christ ... in whose name and spirit we pray. Amen.

Reflections

Oh nuts! This is one which, looking back on it, I wish I had not led at all ... or at least had been able to see it from this later perspective and made a few changes. What bothers the most is the little "commercial" thrown in about the committing of "time, talents and wealth" ... which may be alright to do in other circumstances, but seems sort of unfair when sneaked into the intimacy of prayer. I struggle with this, and bristle when I see others doing similar things. Was I aware of an ulterior motive then? Or was this entirely innocent? I don't know. Also, without fairly deep reflection and/or dialog this could seem like a put-down comparison, or a discounting of some of others present who may have taken deep and mature steps into the faith. And some who are comparing their teeny steps just could feel belittled. Although this was certainly not intended I can see how it could be taken that way. I don't know. Often I feel I belong among the babes, and once in a while on the fringes of the sage/disciples. I don't feel put-down or set apart in any case. (or do I?, mmm?) But how might others of the flock feel? A bit of time picturing myself in their shoes might be well spent. But on the other hand, too much "navel-gazing" might well short-circuit being able to lead a congregation in any prayer at all. And I must take seriously my wife's suggestion that I may be too much controlled by my worries about "what people think." What do you think?

Reader Reflections

THE LISTENING EAR OF THE UNIVERSE

O God, you who are for us the listening ear of the universe, hear our prayers. We need some setting in which we may feel free to speak our deepest fears, disappointments and needs, as well as those bringing tears-to-the-eyes joys which cry out for genuine celebration. But, God, maybe that's not what we need the most. What we may need almost more than life itself, is a setting in which we can pull up our most tender, vulnerable self and say, "This is what I am most ashamed of; here is the unexpurgated version that I am afraid to share with any single soul I know. I need to know that you can hear that and still love me, 'just as I am.'" Or, could it be possible that there are things I have buried so deeply that I have hidden them even from myself ... and that you are able to see and hear even them! And still accept and love me, "just as I am?" O God, we need some assurance that some part of this big, seemingly so cold and impersonal universe hears our most joyous, "Whoopees," and our most tender and forlorn whimpers ... whether or not we can express them or even realize they are there. We need that, God.

So now in the brief quiet of these moments, we pray you will grant the freedom in each one of us to bring before you what is the most real, right now. (Whether we feel it is accepted or not, help us to know, at least in our head, that it is ... as we listen.) /

Thank you, God, for hearing, for forgiving, for that quiet hug of acceptance, and the call to move on. Now we bring into your presence the names of some for whom we are particularly concerned this day (including ... for some of us ... ourselves): _____.

But you know, God, we must admit that we do not really know what to ask for, that what we ask for on their behalf might not be what is really their deepest need. So today we take a few moments to picture each of them in our minds and hearts / / / / / / / / / / / Now, let us picture loving, Christly arms reaching out and surrounding each of them and us in our needs. We trust those arms of your love to know the real need, and we trustingly leave each one of us in those strong, caring, healing arms of your parental, never-giving-up-on-us love / / / / / / / / / .

And now, God, hear our further question: Why is that we are sometimes surprised to discover, maybe in a news item or an obituary column, things that have been shielded from us even by those who have shared the life of our congregation? If ever it is because they were afraid to speak it for fear of our judgmental eyes and ears, or they really did speak it in words or silences, or absences, or other actions ... and we just weren't listening ... so that they might sense ... through us ... your listening ear ... forgive us. We confess that so often it is so hard to get beyond our own little selves. Could it be that had we known how deeply you have heard and accepted us, just as we are, we would have been better able to hear them ... as a part of the Body of Christ. But for this morning, at least, when we hear: "This is my body ... my blood ... for you" ... help us to respond, "Oh thank you for hearing my need." For it is as a part of the Body of Christ, and in his name and spirit that we are bold enough to pray at all. Amen.

Reflections

Oh my goodness; I wonder if the congregation was really able to hear and follow and enter into all of the ins and outs of this one? I felt so good about it at the time, but was so apprehensive afterwards. Part of the problem, I know, was lack of time taken to really work all of this out, so, though it was mostly written-out, there hadn't really been a sufficient review process. Was it a turn-off for the more traditionally minded among us? If so, was the use of it justified at all? I know that it was appreciated by some, but others may have felt they were being kind by withholding their opinions. (See the insecure pastor fearing that every-one won't approve?) Sure glad Jesus didn't get caught in that trap. But then, don't such fears sometimes push us into a honing process that may be for the good. Well, yes, it was thrown together too fast, but sometimes that just has to be. Probably this is one of the tight-ropes a conscientious pastor must walk. But God help us if we ever stop asking the questions.

Reader Reflections

INTERWEAVING

3/20/99
For the Kidney Foundation "Spring Swing" … at the Flamingo Hilton, Las Vegas (a fund raiser with silent auction, banquet, a swing-band and dance instructors to help any who might want to give it a try)

Introduction:

Gotcha! Now don't look so surprised. This prayer is on the program, and there you sit, so for a few moments I've "gotcha"… (although the thought has crossed my mind that at any moment the ACLU may slip in to tell us we can't do this). But you relax and I'll worry about that … while I ask you to walk with me through a memory. Feel free to close your eyes for this if you wish. It's a few years ago and we are just entering a church to attend the funeral of an old friend. Stepping in we hear the strains of the sweetest "big band" music playing from the balcony. You see, my friend was a member of "The Jazz Assemblage," one of the finest swing bands around, and they'd come to see him off. The service goes on to weave together the themes of Marshall's life and faith, including his love for that music … and the moment the a-men of the benediction is spoken, there begins from the balcony the strains of, "There Will Never, ever Be Another You." And I cry. I cry, thinking, "Wow! that's true … and that music is a part of who he is. His Creator has woven that in with the many other building-blocks with which my friend has been continually created, new each day." And I thought, "Me, too. The music of my era is a part of what I am made of. And that's good."

So, now … on behalf of all of us here I address You … You, who has brought us into being … won't you please accept our thanks for the way you have somehow woven our lives together in the process of creation, and brought us together here in these moments, as in the peace of evening we slow down from the mad pace of the day and begin to breathe a bit more peacefully / / / / / / /. Would you remind us once more of that interweaving through which you cause each of us to take in the food created from the sun and soil … and breathe the same air … and fill our souls with the music, which entices our feet to dance … until we are all connected-together-parts of the one great, whole earth … so the joys and hurts of each one of us must really be the joys and hurts of each of us. How easily we forget that. …Yet no one would be here if it were not for our care for one another. So help us this evening, we pray, to really, consciously, enter into a swinging celebration of life; of our need of and care for one another. May we freely and joyfully use these moments as a celebration of the wonder and miracle of life. Life together at the bidding of you, our Creator, to whom we pray. A-men

Now, … don't just eat …<u>dine</u>! Toast one-another. And may your meal be a feast!

Reflections

I was surprised at the number of people who came up to me later in that Casino-ball-room to say things like, "I have never been very religious, but I really appreciated that as a beginning of our evening." That felt good; but my thanks were always underlaid with questions in my head: How does this form of prayer come across to the more orthodox, who may feel their participation in it may compromise the specifics of their faith? Does it really (as I hope) open doors for the "never been very religious" to consider that they may have been turned off by narrow stereotypes of what faith is all about, and to look for meaningful expressions … or at least questions … of faith in their own lives, and in interactions they may have felt were "only secular?" Maybe they will discover they are more "religious" … or at least more "faith - full" than they had thought.

I honestly think we should consider the sensibilities of those whose orthodoxies may cause them to hold themselves back from what seem to them to be improper celebrations. But I am not sure to what degree. Is such participation in such genuine celebration, as a way of funding an essential social agency, a seeking of some lowest common denominator, or is it in the tradition of the Apostle Paul saying on Mars Hill (very loosely paraphrased), "I see that you are very religious; might I suggest a few fresh ways you could look at that?"

Reader Reflections

THANKFULNESS

Can you know, O God, how difficult it is to really celebrate this season of Thanksgiving ... or even to pray a prayer of thanks ... without sounding as if our faith in you must be conditioned on our receiving what we judge to be "good" things? Can you know?

It is wonderful to be able to shout, today, "Thank you!" for the news, just this week, that Ruth is in total remission, but as we do this ... well, there's the question, did we think to give thanks, while the disease was raging, for the knowledge that you were a presence to her and would be using the whole experience for a growth of soul that could probably have come in no other way? We will give thanks for our food this afternoon, but how much will this contain the unspoken prayer, "If so much of the world must be starving, we are thankful that it isn't us." O God, is that really our prayer? It is so hard to let go of our little selves enough to be able to speak to, and listen to, the hugeness of your eternity. And how can we enter into your eternity without letting go of our grasping at the tiny, anchored to the earth, temporal things that make up so much of our lives? But, then, you've given us the freedom to do that anyway, haven't you? In so many ways, if we will but listen, we hear you saying, "Come to me as you are, for I accept and love you in your weakness as well as your strengths." So thank you for such wonderful freedom ... as like a child coming to parents to tell them how much we would like to have a shiny new bicycle, when the parents know that would not fit into the budget, and we are yet too young to have a bicycle anyway ... we come knowing that you want us to express ourselves to you, as we need the intimacy of such communication, irregardless of our degree of maturity at the moment.

So, thank you, God, for setting us free to be who we are right now ...as you continue to draw us into who we may become. And now, as we look around us with our closed eyes, hear our thanks for this wonderful space, both physical and spiritual, which is the building, the sanctuary of the community which is our Church. Where else in this frantic frenetic corner of the world, can young and old, wise and foolish, rich and poor, come together to cry and laugh and sing together without having to wear our Sunday-faces-or-clothes ... or our halo's ... and somehow sense you in the midst, helping us help one another to come to better know, both each other and you, the Helper and Reconciler and Lover.

Thank you for this wonderful day and all that it holds for us. And thank you for being born as a child into our lives so that we may know it is OK to get where we are called to be ... by growing up. In the Spirit of the Christ. Amen.

Reflections

Thanksgiving is, for me, one of the most difficult seasons for prayer—both corporate and personal. Oh yes, I can glory in the many things for which I am thankful, and that is good. But the question continues to arise: Is the reason for the gratitude the appropriate reason? Ideally, I would treat the subject of thanks much like Paul treats the subject of hope in his well known, "Hope that is seen is not hope." So profound. So the hope for our ideal, and possibly "bargained for," future fulfillment may miss the point entirely … for the hope of which he speaks must be the trust which says, "there is always hope, even though I know it may not come to pass in the form which I would have chosen." It may not be anything I have seen … "visualized" … at all, because of the shallowness of what I encourage myself to "see." Isn't it interesting how much the context of our praying may come from our own pasts …as the bicycle reference relates to my own depression days memories? And I often wonder how much the congregants may be led by the mind-pictures of the prayer-leader, to draw up their own very meaningful mind-pictures from their own lives. How, really, can I help to facilitate their own imagery through the sharing of my own?

Reader Reflections

GOD OF THE MOUNTAIN

(Sung by the prayer-leader – "God of the mountain, God of the hill; Show us your vision, Teach us your will.") O God, some of us remember those "mountain .top" experiences when you were somehow, so close and alive to us; and we praise you for them ... as they have come to us as youths at camp, or on the mountainside or the sea-shore, or through seemingly divine relationships while young or old. They have changed us, shown us visions to live by, overcome what had seemed such a fearfulness or dreariness of existence.

But we forget. Sometimes we look back and say, "Oh it was just an emotion of the moment." And so much of the time we live out our lives either in deep dark valleys, or on a level plain where we are afraid to feel ... to feel either the exultation of your presence, or the pain of our lonely hurts and griefs. And, honestly, God, some of us must admit that we have never ever been with you high on any kind of mountain top where we might have heard the promise of your Presence ... ever after ... even in the dark valleys we know we must, sometimes, walk ... alone ... or with others.

Forgive us, God, where we have not heeded your beckoning to us to climb high, and to see and hear. Forgive us where we have been unable, or simply refused, to draw near by trusting and entering into fellowship with those who have. Forgive us our skeptic hearts, which keep us closing in upon ourselves and failing to walk "the way" with you, and with the sisters and brothers you have given us as companions on "the way."

But then, O God, could it be that we have been, somehow, drawn to this place so that it ... this place ... might sometimes be for us the mountaintop of the experience of your presence? Could it be that you have tried to draw us to mountaintop after mountaintop, and have spoken, but we have not heard or have heard and thought it was only the wind? Could that be? Then help us, we pray, in these moments (among the people and the symbols of the faith which beckons us) to "be still and know your guidance to be open to ... and begin to recognize ... whatever you may have for us. And help us to know ... here together ... that amazing promise: You are forgiven; I accept you and love you just as you are. In the name and the spirit of Jesus, the Christ, we gather and pray. A-men

Reflections

Is there a danger here of setting up some people to feel that they are inferior to some sort of "spiritual elite" … "spiritual athletes" … who have experiences which set them apart? If this is a valid danger, is it worth the risk to open up the possibility and invite them into the experience at this time and in this way. At this point I believe it is, but still with the recognition that some may feel left behind … and might possibly just opt out. How could we extend an invitation like this, but in a way where they would more nearly feel our sense of inclusion … of them? I'm still working on this one, and feel now that if I had been critiquing then as we are proposing now, there might have been an appropriateness built in, which is sometimes missing here.

Reader Reflections

BEING A PEOPLE

Oh sheltering God, you who promise to be our fortress and our strength, how we yearn in these moments to experience your presence … that strength and protection … not just as a gathering of individuals, but as a called-together congregation, as a people called from the community to experience the wonder of knowing in our bones that as we relate to one another in the bonds of your forgiving, sheltering love, we become so much more than just the sum or our parts. Help us, we pray, to not just sing and pray about, but to experience those ties that bind so warm and close. Like we have experienced the warm hug or handshake of those in whom we have opened ourselves in family and community.

Of course we have fallen short of the possibilities you have placed within us (as individuals and as a congregation), so now we want to be open to allow the flow of your grace and love to wash over us and through us to one another until we begin to accept it as naturally as the air we breathe …so we might live as forgiven and forgiving people, willing to live lives of risk and adventure, in the knowledge that we have been set free and have nothing at all to fear. But God, you have put our congregation all over the map, and we will need your vision to see ourselves bound by ties so much more than physical nearness: Those who are home-bound and alone, those like _____ _____, trying to sort out what a diagnosis of _____ may mean to her life, and what kind of support there will be; others doing the hard work of rehabilitation, and those so decimated by grief that they can hardly imagine any future at all … as a part of this same body with others called into positions of leadership who may feel so alone in the unpopular stands they may feel called upon to make. Of course we cannot all be together in the same place all the time, and can seldom agree on everything, but we thank you for the way you move us beyond the limits of time and space, and seem to be able to fill in the spaces between us when we would be, otherwise, absent from one another. May they and we somehow sense those one-another ties that bind us in your love … across all of our differences. Then as we who are in this place … this place made more holy by all who have brought .their hopes and dreams here, and haunt it now with their presence … as we break the bread and drink the wine of that loving body given for us, we pray you will help us to trust that you really are our dwelling place in all places and generations …in the shelter of the love that will not let us go … then and now and always. In the name and the Spirit of Jesus, the Christ.   A-men

Reflections

Maybe I am counting too much on people taking seriously the intermingling of time and space and eternity. By stretching out in that direction so far that many may have no idea what we are talking about, will we simply lose them? Or may this not begin to open questioning doors to that which we cannot define, but where they may begin to experience the indefinable in little bits and pieces around the edges? Then possibly we may miss the boat if we do not try to create opportunities for parts of the congregation to join us in reflecting, asking questions about things which very well may now be beyond them, but beginning to percolate up, and then building on the ensuing dialog … maybe some kind of consistent, "post-worship" dialog. What form might that take? That's worth pondering. What opportunities could be structured into the process, so they could enter, consistently, into free and open dialog on those things they may be beginning to sense around the edges, to test them out with other members of the body? Would this kind of corporate praying be enhanced by some way in which the worshipers could enter into dialog, immediately after, with others who had been there (either in small groups or the entire congregation … either with the worship leaders, or without them), so they could question and pursue any emerging spiritual growth which might be rising up out of the process? How many leave without having opportunity to question and hone the process. That's worth pondering.

Reader Reflections

27

GOD OF SABBATH-SANCTUARY REST

God of every one of the many rooms in which we live, we thank you especially this morning for this "sanctuary" room and for all it has come to mean. As we recall the names and faces of all those with whom we have especially shared joys and concerns ... ours and theirs ... we are so thankful to have sanctuaries (places of refuge) such as this and the gifts they bring: of respite from our fears ... peace for the healing of our wounds ... the shalom/peace of your presence ... the trust and comfort that seeps in when those who freely share their strengths and weaknesses and needs gather together like chicks under the protection of your wings (in this place where so many of that great cloud of witnesses continue to hover around us).

O God, so much of the time it seems there is so little peace from the hurrying and worrying and the grieving and the trying to measure up ... and the fearing that we won't ... of the slipping through our fingers day by day of these lives, that some days seem to be such a wondrous gift, and other days such a dreadful curse. How much we need places and moments, and days of Sabbath-rest ... and sanctuary, where and when we can rest, truly rest, from the labor and hurry and worry of it all. How good to be reminded that you blessed and hallowed such times of rest by resting yourself (on that 7th day of creation) "from all that you had done." Could it be that, in some way we may never understand, your rest may need our rest ... that your call to us to "be still and know (in the stillness) that you are God" is somehow a plea to us, saying to us that only when we can finally "be still," when we can stop, and rest and let go ... only then can we begin to see and know how inextricably you have bound us together with one another and with you, and in that know you? ... Only then can you rest ... for one of the goals of your creation is then accomplished? Oh, forgive us where we keep you, unresting, waiting there.

So God, as we thank you for sanctuary moments and sanctuary places, and for your infinite, waiting patience with us, we pray we may be able to allow you to lead us into a stillness that knows; that sees our ties: Ties to those we lift up in joy and concern ... to friend and foe alike ... to a world, including us, floundering in various combinations of self-centered-ness and greed. Help us to be still ... and know ... to at least begin to know you, as you know us ... in these moments while we wait in your presence. In the spirit of the Christ who teaches us to pray together: Our Father . . . . Amen.

Reflections

Once again arises that fear of having tried to sneak a sermon into the "corporate privacy" of prayer together. But does not prayer consist of various forms of "dialog with God?" Looking back on this one it seems to be about equally dialog with ourselves and dialog with God; and I am not sure that these categories can ever be separated from one another. I am aware that some purists who strive for "proper" prayer may miss a stated "petition for forgiveness" section. I had not been thinking of that as this was put together, and it may be a justifiable caution. However, after noting this and going back over the prayer, it does seem that, besides being voiced at one place, the petition for forgiveness is implicit at various other points. I realize that the sense of a God who could ever be in need of our response may be incomprehensible to some, and simply "bad theology" to others, but it seems to me to be biblically justified, and to result in praying which moves more easily from petitional to dialogical. And isn't it through a kind of dialog that our growing understanding of God is, at least for us, the equivalent of our growth in relationship to God? And, as in any lover's dialog, the deepest understandings may often be unconscious or "spiritual" understandings that stubbornly resist being put into conscious, rational words.

Readers Reflections

LETTING GO WHILE HOLDING ON*
(A Pastoral/Congregational Funeral Prayer)

Thank you, God for binding us all together into the community of your people, gathered together through the centuries ... and for now bringing this particular congregation of all of us all together in this very appropriate place at this very appropriate sharing in the transition of Betty Simcox into the next stage of living which you have prepared for her ... for us all. What a privilege this has been and continues to be! Help us especially, we pray, to sense how Betty and we really are a part of that "great cloud of witnesses," which stretches through and beyond time.

You will help us, won't you? ... we know you will ... help us in the moments ahead to continue in our celebration of Betty's life: More tears to be shed, and we need the freedom to share them with one another. Reminiscences are in order, and of course we could never reminisce over the life of one such as Betty without her sparkling sense of humor sneaking into the process, so there will be laughter. Free us, we pray, to honor her and include her in the laughter, which was so much a part of her "trade-mark." And we anticipate your involvement in those moments when we look back and discover that the laughter and the tears have been, so appropriately, blended together into a gift of love.

We thank you so, for the many years you allotted to her span of life in our midst, and for the privilege we have had to share in them. And, especially now, we thank you for drawing us all together, into the fellowship of Jesus, the Christ, as he stands there where time and eternity intersect, and joins our hands and hearts across what might ... otherwise ... have seemed such a final and uncrossable barrier. Help us to sense this "intersection" as we also trust her husband, Bill, into your parental care, with us as brothers and sisters in this family affair. Sometimes such gifts as you hold out to us are almost more than we can realize ... so we have our moments of doubt and fear, and it becomes so important to know that you receive and accept each of us just as we are and continue to gently reach across the barriers we set up and beckon us back so that, eventually, we know that there never was a time when we were separate at all. For in Christ all things really do hold together. All things! So, in that trust we pray this together prayer, and all of our individual prayers, in the name of Him ... in whom all things hold together. Jesus, the Christ; the Lord of our lives.   Amen.

*Permission granted by Bill to use actual names.

Reflections

The pastor prays many kinds of "pastoral prayers" simply because of the pastoral/shepherd role played in the congregation. So it seems appropriate to include gatherings of the congregation other than the usual weekly occasion of worship. It just may be that some members are more tuned-in to hear the message of eternity during such funeral moments than at any other time; also that during times of prayer their "depths" are more attuned to things they might not, otherwise, hear than during other occasions of the spoken word. So is not this a time when it may feel natural to blend these elements together and not have to keep asking the question, "Am I trying to sneak a sermon into this prayer? (Hmm-m-m ... maybe this shouldn't be so much of an issue on other occasions either; could it be that I am merely expressing a personal hang-up when I keep repeating that question? But, on the other hand, what of the times when I have heard that so blatantly done? I'll have to keep working on this one.)

A bigger question for me, now, is whether or not this prayer would have come out differently if, at the time, I had been thinking about the pastoral prayer as "Lover's Dialog." My impression is that it probably would have been at least a little bit different. Hopefully a bit more helpful.

Reader Reflections

WILDERNESS WANDERINGS

Oh God, we have heard your promise to be with us in all of our wilderness wanderings in the desert places of our lives (as well as in our joyous celebrations); but when it hurts, when loneliness sets in, when we thirst for the clear refreshing water of what seem to have been the "golden ages" of the past, we so often turn and become like spoiled children, saying, "I will love and believe in you as soon as you meet my demands and do it as I ask." Forgive us, we pray, for our willfulness. Forgive us for the blindness and insensitiveness to your loving presence, surrounding us still, even when things do not seem to be going right ... for there really is among us: the aching loneliness of those whose relationships just won't seem to come right; desperation fear for health or lively-hood; or dark anxieties about ... well, we're not sure what ... but so many fearsome "possibilities" which seem to be lurking in so many shadowy valleys just ahead. And the fears are real, and they can be terrifying, and they cause our very physical being to tighten up and ache, and trust comes so hard. Forgive us for cutting ourselves off from your promised, loving presence. Your presence even in the desert moments of our lives.

Forgive us, we pray, as we ask for open eyes to see and to reach out to one-another in that warm, vulnerable humanness, which may be one of your greatest gifts to us. Help us in these moments to accept your gift to us of humanness, to embrace it, and see you reaching out to us through one another, even in the desert/wilderness places, which are sometimes a part of the gift. Help us to use that gift, by hearing, and understanding, and accepting, and walking with one-another in the light of your accepting, redeeming love. We want so much to accept your gifts to us, but how can we when, so often we do not even see them as gifts; and we become like ungrateful children at Christmas, turning our backs upon those warm "jammies," just unwrapped, when our hearts had been set upon toys.

So, now, in the quietness and the waiting-ness of these gifted, shared moments in consciousness of your presence, we lift our prayers for one-another. Help us, we pray, to really experience you within and amongst us. Here, where we are not bounded by time and space, help us to be able to look within and see the arms of Christ, reaching out and enfolding those for whom we pray, with whatever is needed the most, as we become sensitive to your enfolding and supporting presence and care for _____

_____

And in the process, may each one of us experience those loving arms enfolding us in our own unique need ... even in our wilderness/desert places ... and then dancing or laughing and shouting with us, in celebration of our rediscovery of your welcome-home-my-child love which has been following us through all of our wilderness wanderings all along ... as we accept your forgiveness for our waywardness, in the name and the spirit of Jesus Christ, our Lord.   Amen.

Reflections

I am really coming to believe, with the opening sentences of the Gospel of Mark, that "the beginning of the good news of Jesus Christ" is a voice crying in the wilderness. Throughout the Bible we see that cycle repeated over and over ... as it is in my own life; and probably everyone else's life. This prayer may miss or go right over the heads or past the hearts of those who have not been introduced to that profound in-sight which Mark expounds so well. I hope I was not "jumping the gun." But, on the other hand, in the hoped for openness of prayer, might not some people be drawn into the realization who have never really "heard" it in the teaching, and may be more receptive in the context of prayer? I think the possibility makes the venture worth the risk. But critiquing this prayer now certainly brings home once more the vital necessity of surrounding the experience of prayer with oceans of biblical teaching and dialog. And, yes, surrounding biblical teaching and dialog with oceans of prayer. I see I am going to have to continue to wrestle with my fear of alienating seekers by exposing them to corporate prayer experiences beyond what we may "understand." How will we ever "stretch" ourselves if we are afraid to move beyond the things we understand?

Reader Reflections

AS ONE OF US ? ? ?

O God, we sing of your glory and pray for your power poured out upon us ... because we are such needy people. There is so much hunger within us and among us for ... well, we're not just certain what the hunger is for, but we certainly sense our weakness and impotence, and we sense that you are the only possible answer for it, the only "food" which can satisfy ... But, God, we just declared together that "you have come into the world as one of us, bringing light and life."* And we have a hard time *believing* that. Why ever would you have risked being one of us? ... at our level? ... partaking of our weakness? ... Or wasn't that really so? ... Could that have been something just made up out of our neediness?

Is it possible that you, who are the pinnacle of all that is, took the risk of entering as intimately as a helpless baby among us ... because you hunger for our love, even as we hunger for yours? Could that be? We're asking you in these moments together. Could it be that you really feel the difference ... the difference whether we recognize your PRESENCE amongst us and within us ... or whether we don't? That you hunger for that genuine response from us? Oh, wouldn't it be something if that were so! Maybe that is part of what our hunger is for. That we need to know that divine, two-way intimacy ... as lovers do.

Then help us, we pray, if we cannot yet really experience your yearning heart for us, to at least respond <u>as if</u> it were that way. Some of those on our respective lists of concern today may be in need of forgiveness, a hand held out or an errand done to communicate to them that they are loved just as they are. We pray that you will nudge whoever of us may be at that point of connection with them, to reach out to you for the light and life you have brought by entering into the world as one of us, and then turn and hold it out for them: from you ... to one of us ... on to another of us ... that each of our hungers may be satisfied ... theirs, ours and yours. And, then, may the number of those who are coming to know you in such a personal way continue to be spread throughout the world you have so loved, that such hungers may begin to be satisfied from Kosovo to Washington to a million hospitals and county jails ... and to our congregation of The Church. Oh how we yearn for open eyes and hearts to see and know what it is you are doing amongst and within us on this very special day in our life together ...as we now sing individually and together this prayer of the heart: "Open my eyes that I may see, visions of truth you have for me. Place in my hands the wonderful key that shall unclasp and set me free. Silently now, I wait for thee, ready my God thy will to see. Open my eyes, illumine me, Spirit Divine."# There is so much we just cannot grasp, but this we affirm, that our praying is in the

34

name and the spirit of that One somehow born as one of us, Jesus, the Christ and our Lord.   Amen
    * From a prior responsive part of the Order of Worship.
    # Sung after the Amen, as congregational choral response to prayer.

Reflection

    This one really worried and worries me. That sense of God's yearning for us and some-how needing our freely given acceptance and returning of the Divine Love … for God to find divine wholeness and completion … that intimacy implied (I think) by "the incarnation." I know that is a big one to swallow for some persons of more traditional orthodoxies. I accept that I may be wrong theologically about that. How much do we dare to slip into corporate prayer those things that seem to one individual to be revelations? Or is that toying with people's minds? I have not yet resolved such questions, but I seem to be led to offer this possibility to my fellow seekers and strugglers in the form of questioning-the-possibilities of prayer. Otherwise I may be withholding from my spiritual family the very things held most dear. And I do try to pose such questions in non-prayer situations, pointing out that I am aware of such difference of understanding, and do not insist upon my beliefs for all persons, but encourage each person to freely share what is dear to them in like manner. Still … I wonder. Entering into the above decision has been the richness of life that has come from the decision to act as if certain things were so, even though I would not stake my life upon their certainty. (Dialog, anyone?)

Reader Reflections

HEAVEN AND EARTH HOLDING HANDS

(Another Funeral Prayer)

So, God, we place ourselves in your hands now in trust that you will help us to, somehow, sense how you bind us to one another ... including to Al ... as you fill in the spaces between us with the love which blesses and returns our souls to rest when we finally begin to let go of those superficial things to which we so often cling so fearfully.

Of course we grieve and shed our tears ... as is appropriate ... for that held-out hand, that "trade-mark" kiss on the cheek, which won't be there for us to grasp and to receive, but we are so thankful for this growing sense that where he goes now he takes a bit of each one of us with him, and at the same time each of us is just a bit different for what ... of each of us ... has "rubbed off" on the other, as You have continued to create us all, not alone and isolated, but together in the crucible of your love.

Now will begin a long period of remembering. And there will be good laughter along with the tears, as we realize anew that our human foibles are also among the raw materials with which you have been creating and continue to create us. And, especially today, we are so thankful for the way you have caused earth and heaven to hold hands ... within and among us ... here in these hallowed moments where the two are so inextricably intertwined (heaven and earth) that the imprint of each becomes a part of our very eternal being. And suddenly our eyes may become open and we may exclaim the "Aha!" which comes when it dawns anew that you have caused Christ to be born within us and in our midst as the divine/human bridge, forever connecting heaven and earth.

So ... now ... help us, we pray, to let go of that which is not meant to be clung to, to rejoice in that which can never be taken away; to forgive any and all hurts among us; to hold out healing hands at the impulse of your love, and, finally, to look back upon this day as the proper celebration of the life of, not just Al Renn, as an individual (though that he is), but of Al Renn, one of us, amongst us ... amongst us in the name and the Spirit of Jesus Christ ... Emanuel ... God with and within us.

Amen

Reflections

How wonderful! How wonderful when these inevitable transitions from the "has been" to the "yet to be" of a person actually take place in the "sanctuary" where so much of the slowly dawning realization of what it is all about has unfolded among those who have chosen to celebrate life together week-by-week, year-by-year. There is a tie among us, which could have grown in no other way. But it is not an exclusive tie so that we congregate together in tight circles with our backs to those who might be considered "outsiders" as they join the gathering because of other community ties to the life being celebrated and "bonvoyaged" in this occasion. I have watched it happen as those from outside the congregation are drawn in to the celebration in ways so that all depart with an even wider and more inclusive sense of "the family of God." The circle has not shut them out, but draws them in.

What an awesome responsibility it is to attempt to pull together the people and the possibilities which God's universe has drawn together in one place that all may … together … prayerfully celebrate, not only the particular life, but each person's involvement with the life and community in which that life has unfolded, blossomed, and moved on, carrying so much of it along into the what-is-yet-to-be. Never yet have I fully risen to such an occasion. But what a joy to try … on those occasions when the eternal perspective is up front … as compared to those dreary times when the best one can hope for is to comfort a grief which has nowhere to go. Incidently, this was particularly meaningful because of the cooperative presiding by three pastors and former pastors, as well as the others from the community.

Reader Reflections

IT'S THURSDAY AND THE NIGHT IS DARK
(A Maundy Thursday Prayer)

We bring so much emptiness, O God, into the presence of your fullness in this very special season in this very special place. Among us we have so many differing reasons for being here, and we are so different from one another. How have you managed to reach inside each of us, as different as we are, and to draw us all together, here in this place, in the quiet of this evening? Though we are trying to trust that in Jesus Christ you have come to us and entered into our lives, the trust is probably more a response of the heart than of the head ... "something" in our hearts seems to be calling us to really, seriously, walk this road to the cross with our Lord, but our heads, the body-part of us, which can be so tired at the end of the day ... keep us from really, fully, walking that walk. We find ourselves being drawn into the body's ever-ready escape into sleep, in spite of our Lord's plea not to be left alone, and we find ourselves drifting away ... or are we really bailing out ... far short of the cross waiting there for him.

Yet here we are with this hushed sense that it is really Your Presence, O God; charging the atmosphere ... apparently accepting the shortcomings of our humanness and using these moments to draw us into Your Body here, the Body of those who will trustingly participate in the giving and the receiving of the bread and the wine ... receiving and taking into ourselves his gift ... a gift of body and blood ... the gift of that part of him which is exactly the same as that part of ourselves. How is it that though we continually fall away, you continue to enter into our spirits and our bodies, making them one and drawing them into yours. In the light, we had decided to accept that you were there ... and then we discover you were there in the dark as well. And how is it that we begin praying to you, God, and, somehow, slip into referring to him (Jesus) and you interchangeably? How come? So much mystery in it all.

Oh God, we need so much to be able to open our lives, our very being, body and soul, to the healing, saving mysteries which we celebrate tonight. Please help us to accept you as you accept us. Please enable us to look within and find you waiting there; then to turn and look without, as your arms and heart use ours to celebrate with those who are rejoicing and to enfold those who are hurting (as_____ _____, and the family of _____, and those in refugee camps throughout the world you have so loved) ... to somehow enfold us <u>all together</u> into the life of your dying love. Still we wonder. We have come here to wonder: When we think and speak of the "we" experience all the way from the upper room to the Garden of Gethsemane to the Cross and then that empty tomb in a hillside ...is it your love, God? ... or the Love of Christ? The best we can do is to wonder.

And to wonder how much you are with us in the wondering. Oh … oh … Yes! … Oh, Thank You! … Yes!   Amen, Amen and Amen.

Reflections

The word "reflections" certainly seems appropriate here. That's what the congregation was gathered to do: Reflect and Wonder. So the intention here was to have "pastoral prayer" which would serve, also, as <u>input</u> into the Maundy Thursday service of Communion. Part of the function, then, would be to relate the events of that week in Jesus' life to the lives of the worshipers who now live in an almost unbelievably different world … to serve as a connection point between those two worlds … to make real in the lives of the worshipers the "eternal now," which must reflect and participate in all that was and all that is and all that will be … to draw us into acceptance of experiences which are not limited by our usual understandings of time and space.

Interestingly these questions were not specifically, consciously, in mind during the planning of the prayer, but arose only now in these reflections … I think. Now, that's an interesting thought: I found myself trying to remember and include those parts which were ad libbed into the event … related to but certainly not identical with what was written down … for the atmosphere and the surrounding "community" had begun to open the eyes (and heart?) of the prayer facilitator. So now the writer of the words began to see things he hadn't realized were contained in them, but which in the moment leaped out and needed further elaboration. And shouldn't this be appropriate and be expected?

You know …now that this has come up … this may be one of the reasons that pastoral prayers so often fall so far short. They are so often entered into without such expectations; so the live interplay between the worshipers-gathered and the Spirit … the Presence … may be nudging away, but doesn't actually get expressed. I wonder what would happen if pastoral prayers were reviewed from actual tapes of the service, then re-written with whatever arose in the retrospective contemplation of them, then used again on later occasions? I wonder. They might begin to soar. On the other hand they might fall flat because of the attempt to impose on one occasion (which needed to go in its own direction) another occasion, which had its own life. I would love to read some of the Reader Reflections on all of this. Hey! My e-mail address is: kmborg1@aol.com

Reader Reflections

(Note: You, the reader, have over a full page here for your reflections. You may be saying, "It's about time!" Use as much as you need..

Reader Notes and Reflections

Reader Notes and Reflections

LIKE WATER TO THE FISH

Wonderful, unbelievable God; you who are love without measure and beyond description, we come in the beauty of this day to swim in that love like the fish who isn't even aware of the water because it is so much "always-there." It is easy to praise you as we drink in the beauty of a Michiana sunset, or the crispness of a Fall day, overlaid with the blue of a sky set off by the cumulus clouds of a "football day" … but this is not the proof of your presence nearly so much as being surrounded continually by that steady love which, like the water around the fish is just always there.

So we look back on times of unbearable grief and discover from this other side of it that you were indeed in the process. In our grief we may have either shouted out, or quietly nursed our anger at all that is … but later, only later, we knew … or maybe only in these days we are beginning to know … that you were there, your love feeling the hurt along with us and buoying us up until we could stand on our feet again. You were there! Looking back we begin to see. You were there!

Perhaps only then may come the startling realization that our rejection of a neighbor with what seemed such an obviously "wrong" life-style was really a denial of your acceptance of us in our many mistaken turns … but you were there all along … for the neighbor, but also for us in spite of the hardness of our hearts. Like the unrecognized water around the fish you were there … never was it withheld. (And, come to think of it, maybe the neighbor wasn't so irretrievably wrong in the first place.) O God, you were there! Just as we know now that you are with _____in their hurting, and with _____ in joyous celebration. O God, you are there! You are here!

Forgive us, God, for our many blindnesses to your quiet, patient, persistent presence. We pray deliverance for our fish-like taking for granted of this very context of our lives. We pray for open eyes and hearts, for simple attunement to that context, for awareness as you continue your patient, loving, caring, healing walk with us … until finally, one day we awake to the possibility of walking that walk with all this beautifully diverse and creative world … and those around us will see you in our walk … and together we can leave off being a part of the problem and begin to emerge as a part of the answer. Thank you for being there, even when we knew it not. Thank you for that Presence … in the awareness of which we now pray.   Amen

Reflections

Woops! Am I trying again to get too much into one experience of prayer? As the door was opened for people to look back at times of grating, ripping-apart grief, perhaps some needed more time to let that unfold anew for them in this context. But we blithely jumped into another subject entirely, the acceptance of the neighbor and ourselves. We may have been transitionally impaired. Or transitionally obsessed. How much better to have quietly continued in a way where our griefs could unfold as means of looking back and realizing the presence. Mea culpa ... I think. On the other hand, what about those present who aren't really conscious of having experienced grief of any depth ... or who have never ever rejected a neighbor ... where would they go with this one? And this brings up the question of raising things in corporate prayer that many in the congregation may never have experienced. Is it legitimate to open it to such minority experiences.

But if we don't, how is that minority to grow in the experience of being cared for by God through the prayerful ministrations of the congregation? How will we ever grow into the answers if we aren't free to keep asking the questions. Hm-m-m ... looking back over these reflections I see some valid objections; yet I liked it just as it was. I wonder what that might mean?

Reader Reflections

EXCURSIS I
Middle Of The Night Intrusions
On Praying the Pastoral Prayer as Lovers Dialog Between
The Church, World and God

This is what one of my seminary professors would have called an "excursis" or "extended note." He would explain to the class that these were things which had "come" to him in the middle of the night. Once our class lovingly presented him a gift, wrapped in a small package, and labeled, "Excursis and Extended Note Preventative." He chuckled as he worked through several layers of gift-wrap and finally drew out a bottle of Sominex, an over-the-counter insomnia potion. But we knew that some of the best things this beloved professor had to give us came from those frequent sharings with us of the nudgings of the Spirit, which had come to him in the night.

This incident came to mind as I arose at 3:00 a.m. to put down on paper something about this book that had begun fiddling around in my mind. It would simply not let me go back to sleep until I had gotten up to "incarnate" it … to give it "body," flesh and blood, before it faded out and disappeared forever from my life and being. So many of the seemingly less tangible things of the Spirit seem to do this; when they are not taken seriously enough to be quickly incorporated into bodily "daytime" life before fading away. (Slipping back into the hiding unconscious?) The nudging into life is very reminiscent of times when my wife has nudged and said something like, "Honey, I've been thinking and can't go back to sleep," then told me something that had been on her mind and which seemed to need expression for the good of our relationship, before sleep would, again, be possible. She knew that if she didn't do it, then, it would probably be lost and forgotten; and our relationship would not have the benefit of what "the Spirit" had offered up in the night.

These things happen to the two of us, I believe, because part of the intimacy of the lovers relationship between us is related to about 6 to 8 hours in most every 24 hour day which we spend within touching distance of one-another. Sometimes during this part of the day our awareness of "one-another" (Grk, allelon, check that melodic word out in the New Testament) is conscious; probably sometimes it is unconscious; sometimes a subtle mixture of the two. But the possibilities of couple growth, which arise from both modes of relationship during these hours are simply programmed into our lives, much as the ritual of weekly worship is programmed into the lives of a dedicated congregation. They wouldn't happen if we weren't regularly scheduled into that mode of proximity.

Another Look at the Two-Wayness of our Relationship With God

What had been infringing upon my sleep was the thought that I and my readers would probably need to do a great deal more pondering on questions which were certain to arise at the suggestion that our theology might need to include a larger place for "God's need"—that God might have a need of our response to God's love. Could it be that God really did have a need for us to return the John 3:16-type love, which lay behind the creation and the sustaining and ongoing creation of all that is? Could that be? That God had need of a certain response from us?

And, if so, why? Would not the supposed self-sufficiency of the Creator and the utter dependence of the created, each require an entirely different stance? And for our purposes wouldn't that affect the ways in which we pray ... both as individuals, and corporately as "God's People?" The nudging in the night seemed to be saying that this might be important enough, here in the midst of our journey for a second look: to reconsider some of the implications of that which had continued to arise from our reflections on the prayers ... and that I would probably not be able to get back to sleep until I had done something to begin to incarnate, to give solid, daylight-type, body permanence to that gentle, persistent whisper in the night.

$$* * * * * * * * * * * * * * * * * *$$

As so often when we begin thinking about a relationship between human beings and their Creator, we find ourselves back staring paradox in the face. And there seem to be no "answers" to genuine paradox. When two things ... which seem contradictory ... on courses 180 degrees opposed to each other ... yet are each experienced as "true," what do you do? Well ... usually what I do is to resort to that old friend, "metaphor," a word and image picture which engages experience and comes away saying, "No matter how much I may agree with each opposing definition, this is my experience."

Now, my wife, Mary, is wired so that she can make a bed much more quickly and efficiently than I. For many years we assumed that as one of her usual tasks. But little sighs and remarks from her, during the time when we were crowding into our lives a daily drive for her to continue her education, led me to begin taking up the task of bedmaking, among others, each morning ... in my usual bumbling, uncoordinated way. Among other changes in our lives, that pattern has pretty much taken root. Looking back on it now, I must admit there have been times when my motivation in making the bed has been, "so that she will love me." But on reflection I know that that is ridiculous. If her love for me depends upon a bargained exchange of services ("if you do this for me, then I will love you"), then it doesn't meet any definition of love. For

46

genuine love comes our way no matter how unlovable we may be. Then why am I making this bed? Well, partly it is in answer to the question, "Why not me?" But more and more I think I make the bed as a token expression of my gratitude that there is a significant other who loves me even when I am at my obtuse, contrary worst. And if the definition of love includes the desire for the maximum possible fulfillment for the one who is so loved, then I begin to sense in her some kind of yearning for me to make the bed in order to have that kind of fulfillment. She may have the time now to make that bed, and could certainly do a quicker and better job of it, but my doing it as a response to her love genuinely strengthens our relationship. I am not a whole and complete person if I am not making such contributions. This is a daily symbolizing of my response to our relationship. She may no longer have the time-restraint need for me to make that bed; yet she may have a need (may actually yearn) for me to do this on behalf of our relationship. And the need is <u>basically for my good.</u>

Listen, then, to God, again, as filtered through the heart of Hosea:

> "… yet it was I who taught (them) to walk, I took them up in my arms; but they did not know that I healed them. I led them with cords of human kindness, with bands of love. I was to them like those who lift infants to their cheeks. I bent down to them and fed them … How can I give you up … How can I hand you over . . . . . My heart recoils within me, my compassion grows warm and tender." (Hosea 11:1-4; 8)

Now Mary is not God, but if Hosea and the prophets were right … that the intimacy of marriage is the best metaphor for relationship between creation and the Creator … that factor of yearning on the part of God for our response in spite of our waywardness is certainly a legitimate way for us to picture the Creator/created relationship. A relationship is, by definition, a two-way street. Yearning is a response to the pain of separation. It seems that we will always act out in our freedom with a certain amount of waywardness and reap the separation which results.

So how can our side of the relationship-response ever be free of the pain in the "heart of God" when we waywardly turn our backs. God may not need our love for God's sake, but we need for our love to fulfill our part of a relationship so intimate that the actions—of initiation and receiving—cannot be separated between the two partners in the alternating current of the relationship. And we can best understand that as the yearning of God, as described by Hosea.

Does that make sense?

And, on the other hand, am I, are you, really certain that God doesn't, ultimately, need our love … for God's sake?

THE LAMB, THE WOLF AND THE CHILD

You have held out the possibility of peace, O God, and placed us in a world of turmoil. We bring you this morning our wrestlings with what that is all about. The prophet described his yearning for a world where the lion, the wolf and the lamb might lie down peaceably together, but the fact is that these thousands of years later, the wolf is at the door for a large part of the world, and "the lamb" seems to have been slain in vain. What are we to make of the angel's song of peace among those with whom you are pleased?

If that is the case, then forgive us for our misplaced expectations ... or presumptions. Forgive us and help us to begin to ask, instead, for the calming and quieting of our souls, which comes to us in _whatever_ situation we may find ourselves, so long as we are aware of your living presence with us in that situation. That _is_ what you were promising, isn't it?

Forgive us, we pray, for so seldom being even aware of, or expecting to be aware of you, right here in the midst of our wars and our infidelities and our continual grasping for more, more, more; and then blaming you for not giving us what we had thought you were giving. Forgive us, and thank you for still having faith enough in us (you having faith in us ... that's an interesting thought) ... for having enough faith in us to trust us to finally learn to be partners with you in continuing creation ... so that, when your will is finally done in all the world, it will be because that is what we really want ... because a "critical mass" of us finally wants for everyone to be one with everyone else ... so when one suffers everyone has the privilege of suffering with them, and when one rejoices everyone sees that as an occasion for their own rejoicing.

O God, in a world where a Somalia is even a possibility, we know that somewhere, probably many many somewhere's, your vision has been thwarted. Forgive us for this monstrous enlargement of the little snap shots of our selfishness and grasping for power and wealth instead of love ... pictures that might be snapped day by day in most or our lives. But we don't know how to let go and invite you into the open places that would be cleared for that purpose in our lives. Help us, we pray, to begin—where we are—to change that picture, beginning right now, and to allow the little child to lead us into that peaceable world, the possibility of which you have shown us in Jesus Christ, in whose name we have the audacity to pray. Amen

Reflections

Is it really possible to draw a significant number of people into a consideration of how the really horrendous situations which the evening news shows us across the world may, really, be but enlargements of our own attitudes and reactions? I don't know, but I think we must act in trust that this can really happen ... even if only in little bits and snatches now and then. What percentage of comprehension and response would justify the attempt? Even one person? Even if that one person might be the presenter of the prayer? And the presenter in only a very superficial way, and possibly guilty of "presenting" the whole thing for the gratification of his own ego by parading before the congregation his supposed grasp of larger perspectives which he or she maybe grasps only superficially, and isn't able to commit to much better than those whom she or he is trying to lead in prayer. Also, is it right to throw in a term such as "critical mass" without any kind of explanation of what that term has come to mean? But then, is it fair to deny the one person to whom this might be meaningful, simply out of deference to the rest? Surely we must wrestle with such questions as long as we live and proclaim and pray. Maybe Luther's "sin boldly" should enter into here somewhere. Another thought which crops up in this context is the line with which columnist Harlan Miller used to close every daily edition of his "Over the Coffee" column in the Des Moines Register. No matter what the subject, it always ended: "There is no solution; seek it lovingly." This has become one of my guidelines, and I am thankful to Harlan for that.

Reader Reflections

HIS BODY . . . GIVEN ! ! !

Pastoral Communion Prayer during a Wedding Ceremony presided over by the two participating pastors. The other pastor had just defined the process and presented the Words of Institution. The Groom is Catholic, the Bride is Protestant and they had done premarital counseling with both the Priest and the Presiding Protestant Pastors.

Dear God ... we wonder! We wonder. Did we really hear those words right? Did our Lord really ... at the high point in his giving of himself to us ...use those words: "This is my <u>body</u> which I give to you ... this is my blood ... all this the source of a brand new covenant for forgiveness into which you can tap whenever you feel the need and remember me." Is this what those disciples closest to him heard in that upper room? Is this what we, as a part of his continuing Body in the world, really just heard? So often these words are spoken in our presence, but we don't really hear them. But as we hear him speaking them now, in the setting of the specific love of two people for one another ... their love grounded in his love for them . . . . . .

Oh, thank you for those words! "This is my body, given for you." Help us God, to hear him, and to know in this that the body is not second to anything. His giving of <u>his</u> was his greatest gift of all to us. He said that! This is at the heart of our faith in You. "When we have seen <u>him</u>" (as he said it) "we have seen <u>You</u>."

Oh, thank you for that, agonizingly-given Gift! Now we can know: that the body is not second to anything; that body and spirit are so woven together and whole that our eyes, finally opened to the wonder of Easter Morning; will never be able to see it any other way. How sacred and inviolable are our bodies once we have really heard those words! "This is my body!"

That is what we have heard, isn't it? That is what we are participating in, in these moments, isn't it? If so, help us we pray, to be able to live in the light of it. All of us ... to be able to receive and to share with one another these elements of his body-life, connecting us to one-another, binding us into your family, one and all, in the Body and Spirit of Christ, our Lord. Amen

Reflections

This was one of those occasions when I had decided to prepare only in mind and heart, so that the praying might, possibly, be able to incorporate whatever was happening at the moment in the service. Taken from the tape, some of the implications have been expanded a bit here so that, hopefully, the readers might catch something of what I (at least) was experiencing from the service and the occasion. There was no "change," only brief "expansion."

I am aware as I sit at the word processor that any "theologians" following this might have a field day of pro and con. This is my principle reflection. What I wish is that I could read the "Reflections" of any who do read and reflect. So I will simply leave it at that, hoping that I would have "thick enough skin" to absorb and to learn from what they might have to say.

Reader Reflections

<u>Reader Notes and Reflections</u>

Reader Notes and Reflections

Reader Notes and Reflections

Reader Notes and Reflections

WEAVING THE STRANDS

Here we are again, O God, gathered in this place made special by all we have experienced here together, as something deep within us continues to call us to find times and ways to join with other seekers and strugglers to say, together, "Thank you; thank you for that haunting sense that we really are more than just a bunch of here today gone tomorrow individuals ... going it alone during one little moment of history ... which will simply disappear and will have meant nothing at all." Mostly we don't understand it, but we worship and praise you for those occasional moments of "knowing in our bones" that it all fits together, and that your love still broods over everything that is ... that right now you are weaving together the strands of our lives with the lives of those disillusioned souls in California's earthquake, as they wonder, "What do we do now?" We don't ask you to be with them in their seemingly hopeless moments, for we know that you already are. Our prayer is more that they might *feel* your hurting with them in the midst of it all; your "working for good in all things with those who know and love you," And we feel so much "all in the same boat" as we picture divine, loving-caring arms enfolding the lives and situations of those of our own number, of those more familiar faces we can actually see with the eyes of our hearts and minds, as we place in those arms the lives of _____and _____ _____and_____ _____ _____

Help us, we pray ... as we pray ... to begin to experience ourselves all being woven together, near and far, into the never-completed tapestry of your continuing creation. So we dedicate a portion of this precious hour in this hallowed place to pause and survey a world in turmoil, from Bosnia, to the holy lands, to the ruins of an economic system which just would not work in the Soviet empire, to hospital rooms and living rooms and bedrooms and kitchens here in Michiana where friends we know and friends we have not yet met struggle with the frailties of their humanness. Help us, we pray, to see it all together as our world, and to be thankful for your patient, trusting presence, as you continue to allow us our choices while creation continues to unfold with each of us in the process with you. Forgive us when we simply cringe, and draw into ourselves, and miss the wonder of it all. Help us, we pray, to continue to build with you this "community of faith" into the warm creative "WE" which responds together to your love, and continues to deliver us from the evil of the naked "I" which always seems to fracture the world wherever people attempt to impose their will without seeking out what your will might be ... for all. Amen.

Reflections

Looking back over this it strikes me that this might seem for some to include two worlds: the world of those people who have a history of living and communing together as a congregation; and the world "out there," which we look at and hopefully relate to from the eyes of our one-anotherness. But might there be a third category: those who are really new to the congregation, or who are visiting for one reason or another, with no sense at all of belonging. The "strangers and sojourners" in our midst?

It would certainly not have been difficult to have drawn them in with "hospitality" words to the effect that, as we pray, we are aware of the presence of those who may have been somehow attracted into our midst and to whom we extend the invitation to share in the community into which God has been drawing us.

And this leads to the thought that maybe a sentence or two to this effect might be habitually incorporated into every pastoral prayer. It might be difficult to move this beyond "membership recruitment" to simple extension of prayerful hospitality; but the discipline, I would think, would be worth it. Hm-m-mmm?

Reader Reflections

NEVER ALONE

A service where homebound members were brought
in for their own worship, communion and luncheon

We praise you, God, for this day, and for all the history of love and community and communion at the heart of it. May we accept the gift of this day as one more confirmation of your promises to us. O God, we know ... probably we know better than most ... just how short we can sometimes fall from the hopes and dreams with which our lives were begun. Every day we see anew our weaknesses and foibles; every day we learn anew how insufficient we are in ourselves, and how we must depend upon your acceptance, your grace ... and your promises.

But, God, every day, also, we find ourselves discovering more of the depth and richness of those promises. You have told us that ultimately we shall never be alone, and we look around us today at faces long remembered, as well as faces newly met, and it sweeps across us that we really are not separate, for we are continually created out of those relationships ... as each one of us is a different person because of the shaping influence of those around us ... even though the intertwining of our lives may so much of the time be only through memories and prayer. We're discovering more every day that we really do love one another, at least partly because we are a part of one another ... and we begin to sense that as a foretaste of what the promise of heaven must be all about ... a state of living where we will be finally through with the process of dying (which has been a part of every moment we have known since birth), and will be, finally, living free from all of the weaknesses and selfishnesses which may have, sometimes, in the past, kept us apart. That we are all joined together, in him in whom all things hold together. As maybe we have been all along, but some of the time just failed to notice. Thank you, God, for slowly and patiently and persistently, beginning to reveal these things to us in the mellowing that comes as we learn to lean, trustingly, upon you as we slow down while time speeds up ... and a richness of "solitude" begins to replace what in the past we may have called "loneliness." For now we begin to discover that every relationship we have known has become a part of who we now are. But how can we adequately pray for one an-other as we long to do during these special, precious moments? There would not be enough hours in the day. So how about this?: Let us bind up in prayer what has been going on between us up until now, and agree that this day, itself, shall be offered up in prayer; every sincere wish for the well-being of the other, every expression of thanks, every sharing of ourselves with one another, every thought about those who have preceded us through the years and the centuries, and every aspiration for those now blossoming forth, as families and congregations and friendships continue. Resolved, then, that we will wrap this whole day, totally, in prayer, and place all of it, in your hands, to be used for us all as only you are able to do … through Jesus Christ, in whose name and spirit we pray. Amen

Reflections

Looking back on these written and spoken words I find myself fearing that they might not have been understood and responded to by the worshipers. Partly this fear comes from the (obvious to me) fact that not enough time had been programmed into preparation for this event to iron out some of the kinks and verbosities that sometimes come with the pressure of time. However, along with that, as I type these words, arises the thought that we often sell short the depth of thought which has evolved in some of our older members. That sometimes we are talking down to them while their years of experience have placed them far ahead of us. So I console myself with the thought that, though hurriedly done, this was put together in light of the memory of many hours of pastoral calling upon these people in their places of residence, and that some of the ideas and expressions in it have no doubt grown from insights that they have given to me. Probably more than I realize. And that my interaction with them has been possible at least partly, because I am entering their age category, and experiencing with them some of the "Aha!'s" that go along with our aging …so often not noticed or recognized by the younger members because of a (perhaps defensive) condescension of the young toward the old. It comes to mind now that there might have been real value in programming into the day some time of reflection back on the service to allow them to tell us whether or not the above reflections "compute." However, another of the highlights of the day was a relaxed luncheon served by members; and it may be that the natural interchanges there were more valuable than any other "naval gazing" we might have tried to program in.

Reader Reflections

THE NUDGE FROM WITHIN

Dinner Invocation at the Kidney Foundation
Annual Fund-Raising Ball at the Orleans
Casino Ball Room, Las Vegas, NV, 1/10/98

Oh, you who are the loving heart of the universe, you who breathe into us the breath of life, and so relate us to one another that our very humanness depends upon that connection; help us to slow down now for these few brief moments so we can really be here and allow our hearts to be opened to our need for one another. Help us here, in the quietness of evening, to relax from the breathless rushing here and there which makes up so much of our busy week, to unkink from it all; to slow and deepen our breathing / / / / / and to let go of the rush and confusion. We need that so desperately / / / / /. Now ... in this unfamiliar quietness please accept our thanks for the many miracles we take so for granted as we breathe - in / / / / and out / / / / - the air which sustains our lives and connects us so intimately to the universe which you have made our home. Accept our thanks for the food we will share, created by those same processes, as we continue to be created day by day by absorbing it into our bodies, and thus are so intimately woven together with every other part of creation that we sense our family-hood with it all! All of it! Why are we here, at this place, any way? Probably only because you've been nudging us from within to reach out; to be your hands and heart as concerned segments of this family to which we all belong ... that some of the needs of the hurting parts of that family may be tended with love.

So these are privileged moments; You will inspire us, won't you? ... to really celebrate that family ... to laugh and dance and clap our hands, and joyfully open ourselves to your presence ... there at the heart ... you who have granted us the breath of life, and whispered in our ears to reach out and serve as integral parts of it all. You, in whose spirit we now proceed. So be it. Amen.

A friend (Bruce Larson) says there are three words a person of faith should always be able to say, freely and whole-heartedly:

"No. Yes. Whoopee!"

I am sure many of you had to say, "No" to some things in order to be able to be here tonight. Just join me in saying, "No." . . . . But some-thing must have been worth it to draw you here. Join me in saying, "Yes." . . . . And here we all are ... Let's all say together, "Whoopee!! . . . . . .

Reflections

There are many people who would question the appropriateness of "prayer" on an occasion such as this. Others would accuse me of compromise for not stressing the vocabulary of my own specifically Christian faith. I, personally, experienced this as a joyful occasion, which called for, not a lowest common denominator, but an expression of the relatedness of those from the broad variety of faiths represented ... and, very likely, those who claim no faith at all. Are not such occasions times to stretch people's minds towards consideration of and affirmation of the mystery which defies narrow formulations, yet nudges and prods us to enter into relationship with all that is? What say you?

Reader Reflections

ETERNAL THINGS IN TIME

Blessed and Eternal God, you who forgive and redeem our yesterdays, sanctify our to-day, hover over our tomorrows, and with whom we experience eternal life—yesterday, today and tomorrow—we pray you will accept the grateful adoration of your children ... tongue-tied as we grope to express our thanks for the dawning of genuine eternal life. For we have begun to experience--each day--a bit more of the grace and love and deep-down peace, discovered in bits and pieces as you have been holding it out to us. Not in some dreamed-of future, but in the newly unfolding now!

O God, so slowly we come to know that you have given us each of our days for the living out of eternal things, and we confess that we have used them so often for piddly little concerns that reach seldom further than our appetites and desires and frustrations and fears ... of the moment. Forgive us, and help us to at least begin with this special day which you have given us, to hear deep within us and in our midst the music of eternity ... your accompaniment to the very uniquely human concerns which occupy the minds and spirits and hearts of this congregation ... even on this particular resurrection day.

Is it possible, God ... we ask that question today: Is it possible, that by taking seriously our Lord's Thursday night lament of passion, "Not my will, but your will" ... that by adopting it with him and at least beginning to try to walk with him through it ... he might begin to come alive in this place in ways as surprising to us as that morning three days after was to that other, original, band of doubting and fearing disciples? If that is possible ... and we fear that maybe it isn't ... and we aren't always certain that we want it to be ... but if it is, then please help us to begin to pray, "Let it be, let it be." And then to begin to carry that experience with us into the future.

Help us, then, to so look to Christ, to so experience Christ, to so bathe ourselves in the water of his baptism, that others may begin to see in us who we have seen and been with; so that the fallen sister or brother may experience with us, his forgiveness; so that the lonesome one may know with us his presence and love; so that the proud and haughty might learn his humble servant-hood; so that the sick may know his healing touch, and his strength in the midst of genuine fear and suffering; that the hateful might know his forbearance, forgiveness and love; the dying his life; the bereaved and forlorn, his trust and hope.

Use, us, we pray, O God, wherever need confronts us. Help us to sense in the stillness of these moments, both your will and the giving of yourself, in the way that one intuits the indescribable reality of the nearness and the self-giving-ness of a genuine and trust-worthy lover. May it be more than a passing whim as we pray … in the midst of this celebration of eternity-in-our-midst … as we pray you will raise us up today to begin sharing more consciously and fully the life of him who to know is to know you, the Risen Christ, in whose name we pray. Amen

Reflections

This was fully written out, and was probably shared pretty much as it appears now, many years after. (It was not dated, but comes out of the relatively distant past.) The only thing I can say with much certainty is that it had to have been put together fairly quickly under the pressure of time. Nothing done during the Christmas or Easter seasons was ever done "leisurely," for there always seemed to be the sense of pressure to squeeze in more and more each year. Hopefully I would know better now, and would allow more quiet and silence in my life for the entrance of "The Eternal," as asked for in this prayer.

Reader Reflections

THE ENFOLDER OF DARKNESS

O God of light. You who save us from stumbling in the dark alone; each one fearful and distrustful of the other, as we attempt to defend our own turf ... enable us, we pray, to see those ties with which you bind us to one another ... help us to trust across those differences among us through which you have gifted us with the wonderful, colorful, infinite variety of your creation ...all of it! Never same-bound and boring in its sameness. Forgive us, we pray, the walls we continually throw up between us; forgive us the dark corners we create where we hide in defensive fear of being contaminated by our brothers and sisters "otherness." Forgive us for missing—so often—your big gift of oneness with all that is, as we cling so tightly in the darkness to some small part of it, so we can call it "ours," and pull it in upon us. O God, you who enfold and embrace the darknesses in which we hide, you who have made even those darknesses to be a part of your creation, so that we may have the freedom to choose between the dark and the light ... you who enfold, and brood patiently over, the darkness, and wait like a breath-held parent of daughters or sons out trying their wings on a date ... we pray for your continued patience to wait for our emergence into the light of your creative, health-giving, inclusive love ... if and when we so choose. Forgive us our flirtations with the darkness. Forgive us and continue to assure us of your patient, waiting presence.

Forgive us, forgive us, forgive us ... and hear now our prayer together, and our prayers as individuals in the silence of these moments:

For this congregation, our at-home part of the many faceted Church (Community of Faith) which spans the world.

- For that whole church ... in its infinite variety . . . . .

- For multitudes of refugees, cut off from the peace of what may have once been home ... or never ever having known the warmth and the light-in-the-window feel of "home."

- For any who may feel that they are refugees from this congregation because of misunderstandings ... or neglect . . . . For those who are ill or fallen, or falling out of relationship, and in need of your healing touch . . . . .

O God, as you enfold and brood over the dark places of our earth, help us in the silence of these moments to picture in the eyes of our hearts, loving Christ-like arms, the human embodiment of your love, surrounding and supporting and wooing those we love out of any darknesses in which they

64

may be cowering ... and into the light of your presence. And should there be need of our hearts or arms to serve as the link with you, won't you please nudge us to go ... and do, or just **be** ... as a sign of your yearning presence, in the spirit of Jesus, the Christ, and our Lord. Amen

Reflections

I don't remember this having grown out of any deep, theological reflections about whether or not God might have a "dark side," as God's creation so evidently does. But looking back over it now, there it is. Somehow we've got to grapple with this in our life of faith together, and it just may be that the most helpful, and fruitful way is simply to put it in the context of "wondering" prayer. I would hate to have this one reviewed by a theologian, particularly one with any Jungian-type leanings. As I reflect retrospectively on it I am trying to think of other ways or contexts which might have been better for individuals and the congregation to see their dark side and begin to include their sense of it in their dialog with their Creator/Lover/God. And I don't come up with any. Once again it seems like Hosea reviewing his life and relationship with Gomer and hearing in it the yearning heart of God, unwilling to cancel out the great gift of freedom, and therefore willing to bear and wait-out the pain of the separation until the relationship may sometime be renewed as an act of free choice. Is God's "enfolding the darkness" a legitimate way of expressing this from our side of it ... in prayer. I wish I knew. If there is a better way, I wish someone would explain it to me. Now I regret that the prayer did not include an enthusiastic "Thank You, God, for your great gift of darkness!" What do you say?

Reader Reflections

65

A PLACE OF FORGIVENESS AND
TRANSFORMATION

O God ... you who we call, "God," because no name could ever wrap up in a tidy definition who you are ... you who we can never explain or describe, but who we "experience" ...in the mystery of a starry night, or as the presence that enfolds us by the bedside when the death of a loved one begins to be transformed into a sense of a new birth, which we had not expected it to be, but which draws us on and gives new meaning to our days ... you who somehow manage to grow love in the midst of our living and dying together and to be the go-between who binds us together in a shared love which turns out to be ... well to be ... You ... that "I Am" Presence. Forgive us when we forget that you are the Heart at center of it all, and absent-mindedly make you trivial and optional, by living as if you were not there ... there in each moment, breathing life into the plots of the stories lived out in each of our lives ... and in our life together. O God, we so much need your help, your nudging and pointing and encouraging us to really see one another through your loving, forgiving, life-giving eyes ... enabling us to pass on your blessing to those we might well judge if we did not recognize the struggles by looking at them through those "I Am" eyes ... which keep bringing us to see how much we are alike in our human frailties. Help us we pray, to be able to see ourselves together, as each Sunday we respond as prodigals to your party-invitation, and see you running down the road to meet us in our return from our wanderings, gathering us all into the celebration. No one left on the outside, looking in. You know that each one of us drags along so many hurts and failures, and we need a place like this where they may be forgiven and transformed in the crucible of your love ... which without you in the midst would be so far beyond us. So help us to forgive with your love ... and then to celebrate the forgiveness ... forgiveness of them ... forgiveness of us ... as you hold it out for us to receive and celebrate in these moments.

By your spirit in our midst during the times we share together, help us to lift into that Presence the special needs of those whose concerns we feel in this moment (as each one of us in the silence pictures within those whom we would enfold in your care). May we see those arms of love reaching out around and enfolding, as we look within.

And now we place ourselves, and those for whom we have prayed, right in the midst of this unfolding time of worship and communion together ... and pray you will reach into each life with the assurance and meaning that we so long for if we are to really live in the spirit of the resurrected Christ ... as he teaches us to pray together: "Our Father, who art in heaven, hallowed be . . . ." Amen

Reflections

One of my major frustrations has come from looking out over the congregation and having the sense that, no matter how much we have planned things so that the major goal of the service of worship is to communicate a sense of living Presence, and to invite them all in … probably the majority present are saying to themselves something like, "I don't know how this part fits in, but of course what they are saying is that we'd better shape up or we are going to be in trouble with God! 'cause that's what it is all about and we are here to fill some of the requirements.'" So when I look back at something planned … and invite us all into the mystery of that loving Presence … I often wonder if church leadership which has settled for such requirements just might fill a more positive role in the community. The phrase, "Settled for that," probably sounds sort of condescending, but it may be that those who fill that role and fill it well have learned a kind of realism that I have not yet accepted or fully understood.

Pragmatically, this kind of pondering leaves me more determined to find a better mix in pastoral prayer … in the entire service of worship, actually … so that there is something for everyone, and all kinds of seekers at many levels of growth are ministered to. Looking over this one, I can't help but feel that maybe I did it too much "my way," as "old blue eyes" used to belt out the song. And I can hear my wife at times in the past, saying, "I think, maybe, you weren't listening to them very well." And I can only ask the reader's pardon for the complexity of phrase, which becomes so evident in the reading … but which, I am almost certain, was more easily understandable with the pauses and inflections of the spoken presentation. Forgive me, dear reader; forgive me dear God!

Readers Response

EXCURSIS II
"I Don't Do Weather"

One of the collateral duties which I really enjoyed while Director of Pastoral Care at the General Hospital was the writing of a "Pastoral Ponderings" column for the weekly EMPLOYEE NEWSLETTER. One of those ponderings from the past began coming to mind during the night; sort of nagging me about the recalling of these prayers. I looked it up; and here is what I had written:

A fellow employee (apparently reflecting one of the common conceptions of "what in the world might be the function of a religious professsional on a hospital staff")* waved to me in the hall and said, "Hey, why don't you do something about this weather?" I replied, "I don't mess with the weather." That reply grew out of memories of an incident from 1962, when I was a pastor in Sioux Falls, South Dakota:

On a Saturday evening in January it was just beginning to snow when I ran into some members of my congregation in the Red Owl super market. They jokingly asked, "Are you all ready for tomorrow morning?" In the same spirit I replied, "No more than I am ready for tomorrow morning, I am going to go home and pray it snows so hard we can't even have services." You guessed it; it snowed 34 inches overnight, closed every church in town, let up for 12 hours, then snowed every day until March. It broke every record in a part of the world which already had some pretty impressive records for snowfall, and I spent the rest of the winter saying, "I didn't do it; honest; I was only kidding!"

But had I "done it," it would have brought up some interesting questions about prayer, wouldn't it? What is a legitimate subject for prayer? Is asking for such specific things or actions OK in any relationship one of us might have with the Creator (and Lover)* of us all? How specific? What does it do to me when I center on requests for me or others which, if they came to pass, might inconvenience others? ... or when I feel I might have, or desire more "pull" than someone else? Am I seeking, first of all, results ... or relationship?

Anyway, don't ask. I don't do weather.

Or lots of things.

I guess what was nagging at me in the night must have been the perception that possibly the habitual "relationship" focus of many of the prayers being critiqued here might not only have dominated, but sometimes almost eliminated the more "practical" ministry to the world focus, which, of course, is also, important to prayer. Though the pastoral prayers do sometimes include petitions to "do things my way." I've already admitted to being a bit nervous about it. Sometimes, maybe even, apologetically nervous.

*(parentheses not in the original)

We've also said that, following an emphasis from the Old Testament prophets, we might fruitfully use the intimacy of marriage as an allowable metaphor for our relationship to God. This, then, brings to mind some of the nuances between the relational and the petitional intimacy of the dialog of a couple with one another. So I might say to Mary, "Would you be willing to take a few moments to trim the back of my neck before we go to the party tonight?" That's a pretty specific request, but it's also kind of an intimate one. I probably would not ask it of a member of my at-work staff. Also I would not ask it if I weren't willing to take a "no, not today" answer. Certainly that "No" answer must be included in my understanding of the voluntariness of intimacy. But if the answer is, "Yes," then we both accrue several benefits. One of those benefits is that I won't look so much like a slob at the party; an ego sort of thing. But another less evident benefit will likely be the relationship growth that comes when one lovingly does something for or receives something from the other. Similar things could be said about her request that I get out the lotion and give her a back-rub to ease the current ache. Each not only provides a practical service, but, done in the right spirit, may enhance the relationship.

But Mary may have promised to do something for one of the grand kids, and figures that will not allow enough time for the neck trim. One of my little hang-ups is a real tendency to avoid anything that may impose upon another person … to avoid making them uncomfortable by having to refuse what I ask. I might not have even asked about the neck trim for fear Mary would feel bad if she had to refuse me because of her commitment to the needs of others, or possibly because she knew I really didn't need the neck trim. Could it be that some of my foot-dragging on including such specific requests when serving as the congregation's connection in our dialog with God, is related to that little idiosyncrasy in my nature? (As silly as that sounds when I listen to it now, that would be like saying, "Don't ask for something that may need to be denied, because this might make God feel bad, and you wouldn't want that; now, would you?")

Looked at in another way: There was a time when I was a child during the depression …when I wanted a bicycle. I wanted a bicycle in the worst way. It must have been terribly difficult for my parents, for at first I wasn't old enough for a bicycle, and later there simply was no money for one. But I kept asking for a bicycle. I know my parents agonized over this. But looking back now, I realize that our relationship must have been enhanced by my asking for that which it was not right at the moment (for reasons I had a hard time understanding) for me to receive. To begin with, my asking helped them to know what was in my heart. (Though they may have already known; once I had asked, then I knew that they knew it.) My parents went out of their way to take me fishing and do other things that were possible, which I still remember. And when I finally did receive that treasured bicycle it came from my grandparents, enhancing the relationship to that part of the extended family.

So, one of the messages this little excursis communicates to me is that, if you are one who has the responsibility of helping a congregation find its way, you might be wise to check out some of your little psychological quirks which might be a stumbling block in the way of leading them to a mature, and well rounded experience and expression of faith. Had I done that, possibly even to the point of going for some consistent personal counseling on the subject, we might have been blessed with a more well-rounded prayer experience in our corporate worship.

Also, had I been doing the critiquing operation then, that we are doing together now, this little insight might have surfaced back then in the process, and led to both personal and congregational growth and maturity. That old Pennsylvania Dutch aphorism seems to apply: "We get too soon old, and too late smart."

Nevertheless … I still don't do weather!

Reader Notes and Reflections

Reader Notes and Reflections

GOD OF ALL CREATION

O God ... God of all creation ... can you possibly know how hard it is for us to love all of that creation along with you? We hear your call to love the world as you have loved it, but, honestly, how can we? You have brought each of us into being with such different backgrounds, so some end up bold and up-front, and others more timid and retiring. Some would worship with pipe organs and Bach and others with guitars and synthesizers and Avery and Marsh, or the Gaithers; some with quiet prayer and silences, and some with tongues and raised hands; some in the quietness of silent presence together, and some with dance and hugs. So many temperaments, and colors, and traditions, and life styles. We just can't help being the way we are, and so often those others so grate upon us. Why can't they see it our way? It would be so peaceful if we could just each spend our lives with those like ourselves, and not have to worry about the others at all. Why have you done this to us?

O, Forgive us, God, where you have blessed our lives with variety and change and growth, and all we want is to pull in upon ourselves, and feel safe and secure and "right" in our sameness. Forgive us, we pray, and keep drawing us out into journeying and trust and adventure and grateful identity with this exciting, never completed world of yours. And ours. Help us, we pray to love and glory in the differences; to receive them as your gift to us. Especially our church. When we are tempted to pray, "Just let us be as we are," help us to hear your call to offer those good things that have been with us, as roots upon which can grow and blossom and flourish, those things ... those possibilities ... that can yet be ... that we cannot yet even imagine. Especially as we learn to minister to an ever-broadening variety of people. We pray you will use us, both as individuals and as a congregation, as channels of your love towards those of our number with special needs, and that we will be open to your nudging and prodding us along where you have no hands or hearts available on this scene but ours ... that we will continue to grow hearts to feel, feet to go, hands to touch, and eyes to see ... both far and near. In the silence of these moments we pray you will help us to picture those of our number with special needs, such as _____and _____ ___ and those others about whom particular individuals may be concerned. Now we picture loving, Christly arms embracing these people and situations and drawing them into the folds of your love ... and those same arms reaching out to the unbelievable multitude of the hurting in so many of the wounded and bleeding parts of the world which we trust you have never ceased loving. In the silence, each in our own unique ways, we picture your reaching out. As we quiet our hearts in the inflowing of your love, help us to see! Help us to be still ... and know / / / / / / .In the spirit of the living Christ. Amen

Reflections

How do we offer praise and gratitude for the unique roots and stems and blossoms which have been fertilized and grown up in our own particular (and maybe, sometimes, peculiar) traditions ... and yet, at the same time, not allow the rooting and growing to tie us so close to our own turf that we become shut out from the others who have been given their blossoming in different turf? We walk a tight-wire as we attempt to cultivate the land we have been given and, at the same time, acknowledge the legitimacy of other lands that surround us. Lands which may be needed to fertilize our seeds, lest our lives become weakened through an incest-like inbreeding. It is a tight-wire we walk, for most congregations are made up of a mixture: some who still need the closeness of immediate family for their growth and blossoming, and others who are at the point of stagnation if they do not move out into the wider environment. These thoughts come as I try to think into the situation in which this prayer was born. And more and more I find myself wishing I could twist time around so as to have available right now any future Reader Reflections to help me see how well it might have worked, and what changes might have made it more appropriate to the situation.

Reader Reflections

A PART OF ALL THAT IS

God of our lives, we praise you for the beauty and wonder of your creation through which we begin to see you and come to know you. But, especially, this morning, accept our thanks, we pray, for making each one of us a part of it, and then giving all of it to all of us ... so that we find the meaning of our lives in the relationships we experience as a part of all that is. Not separate in any way.

Forgive us, God, for those times when we forget our need of you and of one another ...and how those two things fit together ... and go about acting as orphans without any need of, or desire for, or responsibility to, the sisters and brothers you have given us in such rich profusion. We know better, but we forget. Forgive us when we know in the heart, but that knowing never quite gets through to the head; or we know in the head, but the heart isn't quite able to warm and give life to the instructions of the head. O God, help! Help us to get head and heart together as we begin to prepare for a WEEK OF COMPASSION* ... that time of remembering who we are by "feeling" (passion) "with" (com) ... com – passion, as if we were inside the skins of those members of our human family who hurt in their hunger, and homelessness, and need.

But, really, God ... week?! We need such with-feelings to be a forever thing, for our own good ... to keep head and heart together ... so we remember every moment of our lives ... who we just basically are. Not orphans, but a part of the family, each one of us loved ... personally by our creator. But even more, able to see the family ... family-ness itself ... loved also by the creator, that Number One parent, who makes us each and all a part of it. Who puts it together that way and invites us ... every one of us ... in.

So we begin nearby, as we pray: Show us the family and friends who are closest to us. Help us, we pray, to really see them and hear them, and not just wait for them to stop talking so we can tell them how it really is. They need to be heard. Help us to listen. Those in our con-gregation _____ _____ do they know they are genuine, integral parts of our "one-another" family? If not ... how come? Our community, nation, world ... how can we be involved in ways that begin to heal the hurts, to bandage-up the open sores and draw us together?

Show us, we pray, O God; open our eyes and hearts to see ... as each of us brings who we really are, to present ourselves to one-another and to you in prayer. Help us for just a few moments to really be silent, to still ourselves, slow down even our breathing, so we are not trying to accomplish, or to say a single thing ... but simply to present ourselves to you, O God, each one a part of the family / / / / / / / / / / / .

In the spirit of, Jesus, the Christ and Lord of our lives.   Amen.

*The name for the CHRISTIAN CHURCH (Disciples of Christ) part of the interdenominational ONE GREAT HOUR OF SHARING.

Reflections

Going back over this material I find myself self-consciously looking at the way so many of the essentials of "good writing" … or "speaking" may have been ignored in ways that would likely drive an editor into a frenzy. But then I think of the many times when this kind of thinking about "professional writing or speaking" may have sabotaged the possibility of genuine, down in the trenches, communication, aimed at a no-holds-barred attempt to draw a roomful of people into meaningful, shared experience. What do you do when you find yourself apologizing for what (in another of today's jargon words) may not seem to be "politically correct?" So I guess I will just try to recognize that as a personal hang-up to be worked around. (But what if this is so professionally "bad" that it causes the book not to be published? To what lengths would I go to deal with that? … an interesting question.)

Perhaps more relevant is the old question of sneaking a sermon (or, worse yet, a commercial) into a prayer?" I don't know. The term WEEK OF COMPASSION was, no doubt, chosen to draw people into a basically faith-full response. And isn't such a response what we are looking for in "lovers dialog?" Yes, but to what degree is liturgy (of which the pastoral prayer is a part) aimed at dialog? Well, if liturgy is seen as "the work of the laity (people)," then probably liturgy is first and foremost dialog. Looking back at the prophet's choice of the relationship of marriage as a basic metaphor; one, like me, who has been professionally involved in marriage counseling, might well ask, "Can interpersonal relationship be as genuine when it is "programmed" (liturgized?) as when it is spontaneous? And I think, from this perspective, it is difficult to separate the two. What happens when the couple deliberately recreates a former experience in order to celebrate an anniversary. Or the counselor suggests, "Why don't you try for a week to act with one another 'as if' the old love were still there?" Maybe WEEK OF COMPASSION type presentations are legitimate parts of genuine lover's dialog prayer. I don't know; looking back I kind of wish I just hadn't done this one.

Reader Reflections

Reader Notes and Reflections

Reader Notes and Reflections

GOD OF THE STILL, SMALL VOICE*

God of the still, small voice; God of sacrifice and love and relationships; God of beauty, including the beauty which sometimes buds and blossoms even out of the ugliness which sometimes seems to envelope our lives, God of the many burning bushes which we so often pass by without even a glance ... because we never (along with Moses) expect to encounter you there: Thank you for your patience with us, where you have given us eyes to see and hearts to experience, and we keep walking blithely by, un-seeing and untouched, because we never really expected to find you on the paths which have become common and dull from our so-daily, so unexpectant journeying from home to work to school, sometimes even to church, to home to work . . . . .O God, hear our prayer this morning for a rekindled faith that if we will just, once in a while even, "turn aside" (from wherever we were headed with our jaws set so tense) ... that if we will just turn aside, expectantly, there you will be, speaking to us from whatever it was that we nearly walked by, all unseeing. Thank you, God, for your patience with us; for coming to speak to us (even though we may not be listening), even through the messes we so often help to make ... thank you for continuing to listen to us. Help us, we pray, to trust that you really do listen; and hear; and continue to speak.

Perhaps it would be good in the dialog which we want our prayer to be, if we were able to sense the ache you must feel as you continue to reach out in so many ways to draw us together into your peace, and yet, as the lover of all lovers, you steadfastly refuse to override the freedom you have given us to choose ... so that any loving response we may make, when made, will be truly ours, and not the choiceless actions of robots, doing as they have been programmed. What a wonderful gift! !. Especially today, we pray: Help us to picture you drawing us into the process of the national election just survived ... so exasperating in so many ways, and yet, looked at over the perspective of the centuries and millennia, so amazing and wondrous a step taken "along the way" or our growth into the oneness you seem to have seen for the world you "so loved that you gave" our Lord and Savior, the Christ, in whose name and spirit we pray. Amen.

*Prayed with Moses' encounter with the burning bush as introduction in the Order of Worship

Reflections

Very likely the "positive thinkers" will consider this a more negative beginning to prayer than they would like. I consider myself a positive thinker, but still feel there are occasions when honesty asks that we lead, sometimes, from our weaknesses and blindnesses; just to be true to who we are ... the kind of vulnerable approach which is sometimes needed in most any intimate relationship, if we expect it to be nourished by open dialog. Though in human relationships it may often be a good practice to begin most dialog with affirmation, had we risen immediately to that level on this occasion, the dialog of prayer would have a different flavor than was intended. (This is all, "I think ..." Actually I may well be wrong.)

Looking back on it now, the final allusion to the current election almost looks like a tacked on political lecture given because of the liturgical calendar of national affairs. Possibly to self-consciously make the pastor seem to be tuned in to current events? If I were doing it now, this might have been left out or, at least, said differently.

Reader Reflections

WHY ME ! ? !
Early January, Dedication of New Leadership

It is easy, O God, to praise you when we are caught up in the wonder of the starry heavens on a summer night away from the lights of the city; or overwhelmed by the electricity of the tentative touch of hand touching hand, with the question, "Dare I trust my life into loving relationship with this other becoming-so-special person?" or simply melted by the smile and hug of a trusting, loving child entrusted to our care. Ah, the wonder of memories. It is easy on a morning such as today when the drive to the warmth and peace of this beautiful sanctuary takes us through a fairyland of graceful, frost-caressed trees. But, O God, forgive us for so often completely missing the multitude of other ways you have so woven our lives into your creation, that we might be drawn to experience you reaching out to each of us through every happening of our lives. We want to be honest in our praying; and when we are we must confess that the seeming setbacks in health, or employment, or relationships often tend to bring out a whining, "Why me?" … probably more often than they call forth the prayer, "Help me, God, to experience from this just how precious is our interdependence upon one-another; help me to sense you wooing me towards the new next-steps-growth-adventure, that, looking back, I may, eventually, see could never have happened in any other way. Show me how my weakness and hurt may finally qualify me to be of strength and comfort to some-one else who may be saying, 'Why me?' as they struggle through similar experiences of their own."

So the more we come to know you, the more we also come to know that you are a God of new beginnings. You have given us a brand new year, now … a time to give thanks for the multitude of growing experiences you keep sending our way … some rapturous; some fearful. Help us in these moments to be able to look back and give thanks for all of them, lest we become bogged down in any "Why me?" evasions of your call to grow through it all. And help us in the same moments to praise you for making all things new (not necessarily all new <u>things</u>, but all things <u>new</u>), as you continue to redeem anything and everything which we are willing to simply place in your hands along with ourselves "as we are."

Now, as we commit ourselves today to those whom we have chosen (and who have accepted) special responsibilities of service and leadership, help us to love you by supporting them in every way we can. Move us, we pray, far from any spirit of judgment of ourselves and others, and towards that spirit of one-another-ness which continually says, "Thank you, God, for new beginnings. How can I fit into the process of your continuing creation? Why <u>not</u> me?

In the name and spirit of him who came "not be served, but to serve." ... so be it. Amen.

Reflections

Wow! Some of those sentences seem terminally tangled up. Ouch! More and more I am beginning to understand the Apostle Paul's seemingly page-long sentences, as he tries to draw people into understandings of things that are pretty much inexpressible. But then, Paul didn't have a word processor on which to work things through. Surely some work on this one could have done some untangling (and I am pretty sure that, in the praying of it, this must have happened "on the spot" ... for no one confronted me with complaints of unintelligibility ... not even my wife. Maybe the more discerning ones had just gone to sleep.)

But this is something that so often enters in. A pastor's schedule tends to draw so many things into it that everything simply cannot be done "decently and in order," and we discover ourselves stretching into places where angels really would fear to tread. How often the clock mocks our best intentions and we are forced to simply go with what we've got. I can't remember how this one was received ... very likely the honest feedback which might help to shape the future seldom comes because of the intended "kindness" of our parishioner friends. And maybe our obvious imperfectness makes us more real and relatable to some of the discerning members of our congregations.

Reader Reflections

GRASPING AND STORING AWAY

Eternal God, we bring these hungry little lives of ours before you this morning with the prayer that we might, somehow, be led into a larger and deeper sense of what it is that you are inviting us, day by day, to share with you. Grant to us, we pray, that the eyes and ears of our deep, inmost hearts might begin to be opened to the wonder of your creation, and of your invitation to us to simply accept it *all* as our family heritage ...as children of, and co-creators with you, the Eternal. Right now we confess that our biggest problem may be that we *do* want it all, but we want it to be *on our* terms. We confess that. Forgive us for our lust after everything, for grasping and clinging and hanging so desperately to things and relationships; for gathering and collecting and filling our basements and our attics and our minds so full ... for storing up for ... well, we're not quite sure for what ...for so often seeming to buy into the philosophy that "the one who dies with the most toys wins."

We pray your forgiveness. But, did you hear our prayer for open eyes and ears? Did we even hear ourselves saying that? Once in a while we catch brief glimpses and hear whispers in the dark, of real "wonders" which we soon dismiss because we cannot believe them to be true. Once in a while there flits through our hearts the quiet message: "My children, you do not need to collect and grasp and store away for the future, for I have given it all to you; it is all yours. It is all yours, *if you will but realize that this is true for everyone of you ... if you will but let go your grasping, rejoin the rest of the family, and receive together your inheritance ... your eternal inheritance, which includes it all ... if you will give up your grasping for little bits of it, so that all of it can be for all of you!*" Oh, forgive us for our failure to see and to hear! Help us to look back on the week just past and, instead of saying, "I feel so bad because the gold medal was won by that one who is not of my country," saying instead, "Oh, I am so proud that this one of my species has won the gold." *The gold is ours, the victory is ours!*

So as we now quietly picture your arms of love surrounding _____ _____in his need, and _____, and we celebrate the marriage of _____

_____and _____ here yesterday ... help us to picture those same arms surrounding us, as one of the congregations of the church around the world; surrounding each of the needs and each of the joys which have come before us, surrounding the refugees who seem to have been orphaned from their homes by the grasping of others of their species (maybe even us), surrounding *all* with your rest ... and with the invitation to let go the grasping of and clinging to little bits and pieces ... in order, from now on, to be able to receive it *all* ... *together* ... as *our* heritage. These things we pray in the name and the spirit of "*him in whom all things hold together,*" Jesus, the Christ and the Lord our all of our lives.   Amen … and Amen

Reflection

What a struggle I have with leading in corporate prayers such as this! For starters, I realize how much of it will go right over the heads of so many who are asked to participate as a congregation. But, more than that, there is the "conscience factor," of trying to lead the whole congregation into something which I do so poorly myself. There is certainly the "projection" factor here; where I attribute to the world something which I find so unsatisfactory in myself; where in looking back, as now, I see my own grasping to collect "bits and pieces" of the whole … see my own fear of the future of our economy, a future where I may not have the resources to survive in times such as these. In reviewing this now I wonder how much of this fear may have been "sort-of" conscious at the time it was being prepared, but I cannot remember. Nevertheless, I love this one, probably selfishly, for welling up from the dark depths into the light of day, leading me to yearn, if only, possibly, half-heartedly for what seems to be so hard for all of us to even see, let alone begin to act upon.

And the question remains: in leading corporate prayer such as this, how permissible is it to let your reach exceed your grasp?

Readers Reflections

WITH NEW EYES OF THE SPIRIT

We praise you this morning, O God, for the indescribable wonders of your creation, so far beyond anything we can even begin to understand. Thank you for making each one of us a part of it; for allowing us to be literally born out of it, so that we are intimately bound to every part of all that you have brought into being. So that we really do belong! Forgive us for, so much of the time, living out our lives as if we could be separate ... as if we could be whole and complete without ever responding to or bearing any responsibility for the rest of this creation-wide home and family in which you have placed us.

Forgive us, God, for what we seem to be doing with it and to it. How can we bear the thought of insane terror wreaked upon people ... as in the towers of New York ... by other people, none of whom even know one-another? How can we bear the thought of so called "revelations" of "Christian Faith" preached over dead bodies from a 50-caliber machine-gun-guarded fortress of captives?!

We see it all around us (when we can bear to look), but we can't see why! Why does it all keep going sour and more sour? Why? Your hand and your heart must be in it all, somehow, but why can't we see it there? ... or find ways we can enter in which might make a difference? Have you caused us to be born into it all for nothing? O God, help us to see! If you really are intimately involved in these affairs of the world ... maybe judging, forgiving, loving, redeeming all at the same time in such events ... it would mean so much if we could just see it all through your eyes ... through the eyes of your spirit.

So, God, if there is any way we can be born into another dimension of this world we have already been born into, we pray for that, right now. We pray to be born anew ... with new eyes of the spirit ... to begin to see the realm of your Spirit in the continual unfolding of your creating, redeeming love, even in such unlikely circumstances.

Sometimes we feel so discouraged, and think our work and struggles are in vain. But then your Holy Spirit revives our soul again. Can you do that once more? ... through the **Presence** we sometimes feel in this place? ... through the spirit of the Christ who joins and enlivens those who gather in his name? Through the breaking of the bread and drinking from the cup?

Thank you, God.   Amen.

Reflections

We were praying about being "born-again-Christians," here, weren't we? I don't think I had thought about it so much in that way at the time. But that's what we were doing, wasn't it? Here in a congregation of one of the much maligned, wishy-washy mainline Protestant denominations? Becoming "new-beings" of a spiritual nature in a world which most of us had thought was only scientifically measurable matter and "things." We were asking for a life, experienceable in the present realization of such a reality, weren't we? Wow! I really don't think now I had thought of it so much that way at the time. (Several years ago.) But would there have been anyone in that stained glass surrounded, pipe-organ-accompanied crowd (sorry, that should read, "*congregation*," shouldn't it?) who heard and experienced it in that way? Looking back now, I think so; but a mighty small percentage of the congregation. So, considering the percentages, is it fair to toss something like this out into such a group of people as a liturgical experience of prayer? Actually, looking back now, I am pretty certain that the congregation included a whole "band," a whole spectrum, of such understandings and experiencings of what it is all about. But that doesn't change the question. Still, now, I feel kind of strange about that ... the feeling that has dogged my steps through so much of my pastoral career ...a feeling of not wanting to appear "naïve" to the sophisticated members who do have a faith, but just, as a matter of course, relegate such things as the "born-again" experience to the crazies out there, the "fringe" people, who are to be loved and tolerated, but not for-heavens-sake taken all that seriously. I wonder how many readers of this material (if there are any) can relate to such feelings? I'll bet, more than I used to think. Maybe it is a part of an evolution of consciousness that such as we could arrive at in no other way. And maybe the world needs a body of people who have arrived at such a consciousness in just such a way ... to minister to just such a developing consciousness.

Reader Reflections

LETTING GO OF WHAT HAS BEEN

God of beauty, and order, and growth, and peace; we come this morning praising you for the way you have made all things beautiful in their time (for those with both outer and inner eyes to see) …for our experience that all things really do hold together in Christ; and for the growth and change which, in our better moments, we know is the only alternative to death … death of people, organizations, political systems … even churches. But we must confess, that, when we are in the midst of the birth processes of growth and change, it is often so difficult to know real peace; so difficult to trust. Forgive us for having to struggle so to let go of what has been, so that we can joyfully allow you to lead us into the wonders of what is yet to be. Forgive us wherever we become unable to see beyond our own ego and will, and begin to believe, instead, that ours is really yours. For, we confess that we have a hard time incorporating the death of <u>anything</u> (especially this earth-bound part of ourselves) into the picture.

As we live through these days of so much change … so much unsettling change in a world of ever accelerating transition and movement and complexity, we pray for whatever it takes to enable us to be involved … really involved … in caring for those who we lift before you in mutual joy and concern; as we do now for_____ _____ And _____ _____ and _____.
We need so much to really be involved, and still know the peace of trusting each outcome to you … so that it may be your love flowing through us to them … and not just our need to feel so important. In the spirit of what we have just been praying, it is so good to know that you know … and bear with us … our frustration, as we enter into our national election process. Though it may often seem that there are no solutions, it is our prayer that you will yet help us to continue seeking them, lovingly, and patiently, and trustingly.* As our congregation of the church steps, sometimes brashly, sometimes timidly, into wherever you may be leading us, we pray that more and more we may be able to feel the excitement of adventure into new territory, new frontiers … to know that you really are leading. O God, in these moments of prayer together we sense that the boundaries of time and space begin to lose their seemingly limiting, frustrating grip upon our lives. Thank you, Oh Lover of our souls, for such eye-opening experiences, for we need so much to sense around us that communion-one-ness and presence of all those who have gone before us through the centuries … of that "great crowd of witnesses" … and to know in our bones that they are still as much a part of it all through centuries and adventures as yet undreamed, as through Christ all things really do hold together. All things! And so we present ourselves to you as trustworthy

stewards of your grace … yesterday's, today's and tomorrow's … in the name and spirit of the Christ, in whom all things hold together.   Amen

*With gratitude for Harlan Millers conclusion each day of his 1960's "Over the Coffee" column in the Des Moines Register: "There is no solution; seek it lovingly."

Reflections

Noting the date of this prayer, November 1992, I recognize how much the frustration of the election process must have been in the background as this was put together. Reflecting in the year 2006, it is pretty obvious that the process will always be with us, and will usually involve us in seemingly paralyzing frustration. So how do you pray optimistically in such a context? Apparently this was one attempt. In reflection on it today I find myself wishing I had tried to express an understanding of "Jesus Christ, the same yesterday, today and for-ever," but recognizing the sense of the sameness of Christ, always including an understanding that he is in relationship to the current situation. How different many people's praying might be if they could think of the sameness as something more than stasis. But how to do that without trampling on some person's trust in the unchangingess of their Lord? Yet I trust that this may be accomplished more readily in a context of prayer than of theologizing.

Reader Reflections

BLESSED, BUT NEEDY·

We really wonder, O God , how we must look to you as we gather once more as a congregation of your people … as a congregation blessed in so many ways beyond our deserving.

We have such an abundance of the good "things" of life;
We live in a land of such beauty, freedom and opportunity
    that it stretches the imagination;
There is health, wholeness, beauty, all around us.

What can we say as we come into a recognition of your presence, here in our midst …
except, "Thank you, God."

But in the face of so much potential for health and beauty, we see so much that seems ugly ..
not well …
and we are a hungry people.

We are hungry for meaning … a sense of purpose and fulfillment that seems so often to elude us,
There seems to be something lacking …
Could it be your image in us,-
Intended, but never attained … or never simply accepted and received.
We sense that you have given us a world of overflowing abundance,
    and yet there is so much hunger … for ourselves, our family, our world,
    and in trying to feed our hunger, so often we seem to devour and destroy one another.

We want our church (our life together) to be winsome and attractive,
like a magnet drawing people to the Christ whom they need so desperately …
like an inviting stream of living water,
satisfying their thirsts and their needs;
but so much of the time this is not the way we look to the world around us …
and not even the way we feel about ourselves.

So we have to say, "Thank you, God, for the possibilities you have put in our midst, And for the small ways that we, now and then, begin to blossom into the potential you have intended …"And then, forgive us for how far we miss the mark, both as individuals and as the community and communion of your people.

Take us and use us, we pray,
and help us to mean it when we pray it.

In the name and spirit of him in whom "all things hold together" …
Amen

Reflections

This one dates many years back. Looking back I wish I could remember the context. Is it expressing a basic pessimism, or just a sense of, time-dated, frustration? God forbid that it was meant to convey some kind of unexpressed anger. Not being able to remember, I must admit that possibility; but hope that it isn't so. My fear from this vantage point in time is that this one may have been, not so much an expression of where the congregation was then, as a kind of projection off onto the congregation of some of my own unconscious feelings about myself at the time. That's a scary thought, but I wonder how often it might be a true element in the leading of corporate prayer.

Surely there must have been moments, ad-libbed in, of reference to current individual, congregational and world needs and celebrations; but, looking back at it, I can't quite imagine where they would have fit.

There was a great line, often spoken by the chief character of the movie, THE GODS MUST BE CRAZY, which comes to mind: "I don't want to talk about it." For some reason, looking back over this prayer, some of those scenes popped into my mind.

Reader Reflections

91

GOD OF OUR RELATIONSHIPS

God of our lives and our relationships; you from whom comes Christ, the foundation stone, in whom all things hold together ... all things ... hear our thanks this morning for the surprising ways you sometimes bring into our lives living pictures of reconciliation and wholeness of things intended, through the fullness of your love, to hold together.

So we celebrate in a very special way this morning, along with our sister, Pat Bell, right now in Korea, the marriage of East and West ... of her son, David Baxter and Hyunju Oh. Thank you for sneaking into our consciousness ... in the first place ... that amazing image of the Kingdom of Heaven as a marriage feast, with all of us celebrating the coming together into intimate relationship of the many, many differences with which you have blessed our lives. Forgive us where so many of the hurts of our world have sprung from our hanging back from such unions, ourselves ... and even hanging back from celebrating them when others, of greater spirit, who have begun to see, and to know, and to enter in ... before us. So, I guess we are asking you to forgive us our resistances; and thank you for your patience as you nudge us along. Forgive us where in our prayers we so often seem to be telling you what you should do, and forget entirely to pray for open eyes to see and celebrate and enter in to what you are so often doing right before our eyes. Thank you for the slowly developing marriage of East and West ... for putting right here in this congregation such a union of peoples through our relationship with our refugee family, the Nguyens ... given us, as such a surprise, to simply be worked out on the spot. Thank you for the CROP WALK, as some of us finally take time out from our feasting in what must seem like palaces to so much of the world ... time out to stop by those starving on our doorstep, and to at least begin to say, "We belong together; forgive us for not noticing you there before." Thank you for your patience as, finally after thousands of years, the feminine and the masculine halves of the world begin, in halting steps, to acknowledge their debt to, and need of, one another ... not as blends and compromises, but as equal sharers of the Genesis image of Yourself bringing creation into being from the male-female essence of who you are. Help us now, we pray, to look around and to really see one another across the world and close to home as we picture in heart and mind those for whom we pray: _____ and_____
_____ nearby; and_____
_____, so seemingly far away.

May "Reconciliation" move us toward those many marriages ...those occasions of celebration ... where the beautiful, diverse variety which you have placed side-by-side in creation finally begin to discover, or rediscover, and

92

"hold together," the gifts they have to give and to receive from one another … In the name of the greatest gift of all: Jesus, the Christ … as in Him you gave-of-your-self-to-the-world you have "so loved."   Amen

Reflections

It is probably obvious the way this was thrown together at the last minute in response to the trip of Pat Bell (the congregation's organist) to share in her son's wedding. It shows the hurriedness of its inception and I make no apology for that. Just as I make no apology for some of the stammering spur-of-the moment ways I have tried to tell my wife how much I love her. They were never meant for publication; and this may be a fine example of the fact that neither were my stumbling attempts at prayer.

Reader Reflections

HEARTS AND HANDS AND VOICES

As we lift up "hearts and hands and voices" "for the beauty of the earth,"* we are really praising you, O God. So please accept the appropriate thanks of this season into which we are entering as our acknowledgment that you have caused it all to fit together in beauty and harmony. Forgive us for the many ways we seem to be able to pit one part of it against other parts of it, and throw up polluted clouds between ourselves and the sunlight of your love, dimming our vision so we cannot see it all together. Forgive us.

Especially do we pray that your love might begin to clear our vision during these many wonder-full days which our part of the world traditionally sets apart to celebrate your love. Help us to rise above the many pettinesses: above the pettiness that may ruin a family holiday-celebration because we are feuding about whether a part of the family spends more time with one side of the family or the other side of the family; above that jealousy which compares what was given to one as compared to another; above the self-centered-ness that misses the point of a time of worship because we don't think "it should have been done that way;" above bemoaning the loss of those … no longer with us … who used to make the celebrations special, in place of remembering and celebrating that specialness; above being unable to "let go" of the work of the world freely enough to allow ourselves to take the unstressed time to laugh and to cry with those who need our presence for the so-necessary sharing between such vulnerable human things as we are.

Help us to see how "big" the "little things" can be and how "little" some of the things the world becomes preoccupied with … and let no "Bah-humbug" disgrace our lips or faces during this wonderful holiday season which has the potential to draw together some of the beautifully diverse parts of our world, into mutual celebration.

So we begin right now by embracing those ties which bind us into this congregation: We pray your joyful blessing on _____(pastor and son) as they join family and friends for "their favorite holiday of the year;" may there be peace and refreshment. Upon the many who will be traveling; upon our union Thanksgiving worship with other congregations this coming Wednesday evening; upon_____ _____ _____ in the hospital awaiting the results of tests; upon _____ and _____ _____ upon so many of our homebound whom we can see through the eyes of our hearts in these silent moments; upon ourselves, as we express our love through our commitments to one another and to you.

And yes, God, hear our thanks for the promise of and the experience of your Presence during those times of hurt when it seems that things "just won't come right," for we want so much for both our struggles and our celebrations to work together for good …to draw us to you until finally we are able to see everything in the eternal perspective of Jesus, the Christ, in whose name and spirit we pray. Amen

*Reflecting two hymns already used in the service.

Reflections

It is really difficult to read something and hear it in the head as it was meant to be spoken. I see that so much in this one, where I would say to myself, "What did that mean?" then would have to "speak" it to myself, and find that it sounded quite different. Something like this probably goes on between the orally oriented people and literally oriented editors or proof-readers. I have to really hope that readers of all of these examples, especially this one, will try to mentally put themselves before the congregation and "speak in their heads" what they are reading. As if they were not reading at all. So often, while listening to a speaker using a manuscript, I have found myself saying to myself, "If only she/he would just pick out some one person out there and try to "punch" what is meant, in a passionate way, directly to them, those same words would come out much differently." Inflections would be more pronounced, little word orders would be slightly varied in the "spirit of the occasion" … it would move from manuscript into dialog and sound completely different. Add the spirit of "Lovers Dialog," and that effect would be that much more pronounced. Ask any wife or husband what they hear most when their spouse is speaking: the word order and grammar, or the tones, facial expressions, meaningful silences … the passion of genuine human communication? So, in pastoral prayer, are they hearing speaker and manuscript like a phonograph needle on a record, or are they hearing some-thing kept coherent and "thought-through" (actually "prayed through") in advance by means of a manuscript … but now transformed by the natural drama of a group of people becoming aware of that promised PRESENCE interacting in a specific moment of connection between time and eternity? You want to tell me? I'm always @ kmborg1@aol.com

Reader Reflections

95

Reader Notes and Reflections

Reader Notes and Reflections

LIKE AN UNBORN CHILD

O God, it is such a wonderful time to be "expecting." We have spent a year praising you and the untold wonders of your creation, our home ... but it's different now. We confess that a year of _praise_ has also been a year of _realization_ ... of how far short the whole world must have fallen from the possibilities of your dream for us. We have prayed, and have been waiting for some sign that your promise of forgiveness for our shortcomings might possibly be true. Some sure sign.

And now, God, we are beginning to feel again something stirring within us; we are beginning to feel pregnant ... to feel that we carry hiding and growing within us, new life; not just renewal of the old, but _new life_, growing from the life of this family of faith, now inseminated with your love ... personalized to wear the flesh of this human family quickened by your Holy Spirit within us. And we are waiting ... and longing ... to see the today-face of the One who already lives within and in the midst of us. "Like an un-born child (your life, O God) grows unseen yet profoundly felt. Insistently pushing and prodding us, enlarging the contours of our lives and our hearts, as intimate to us as our own breathing, yet utterly other, the divine presence waits to be born."* The time of Advent has come.

So, help us, please, not to miss it; not to have to look back later and say, "We didn't know who you was." As the light of your presence permeates even the commercialism of the world around us ... and swells and grows in us who are actively waiting ... prepare our eyes, we pray, to see and to know where you have loved us so intimately as to be born into the backyard-stable-places of our lives ... those places of birth and death; of climbing ladders of success; and toppling off into limbo's of seeming failure; of shining, soaring relationships, and of crashing, crunching dead-ends and the sense of being so-o-o alone.

Help us to trust that you have come into the events surrounding the closing of the 100+ years of our ...crusty and unforgettable ...Clara Brown, and hugged her to yourself; that you are and will be a personal presence in the hospital with _____ and her family; with _____ _____ and _____ and _____.

May the lights and songs of this Season of Advent be seen, not to mock the vulnerabilities of our humanness, but to en-light-en and assure that the seeming darkness does not overcome the light that is continually coming into the world.

Yes, God, it is such a wonderful time to be "expecting." There will be "Bah-humbug's" a-plenty, almost assuredly from people who need most of all to be loved into the expectant family and lovingly led by the hand into the celebration. Be with us, we pray, and help us to see ourselves as bearers of the light of the One continually born into our midst, in whose name and Spirit we lift our prayers. Amen

*Borrowed and adapted from Wendy M. Wright, THE VIGIL, Upper Room, Nashville, 1992, p 32

Reflections

OK, this is probably the time to be asking: How far can we go with the sexual connotations of considering prayer to be part of our "Lovers Dialog" between church, world and God? Will this write us off as "too far out?" Does it need to be masked just a bit more to be palatable, or even acceptable to today's churches? (The word "insemination" wasn't in the original, but was used in a burst of hutspah as this one was typed out ... because that was implied in the original.) Looking back on it now, I wish there had been some kind of reference to the "pangs of birth" which must be anticipated when anything alive and real makes itself known to the human family. Maybe that should have been in the next Sunday's prayer.

And how about the plagiarism from Wendy Wright? I wanted exactly her words, but to have given the appropriate "scholarly" acknowledgement would have broken the spell of the prayer. So by way of foot-note, you see what the congregation didn't. How does one handle such things? Could I ... or should I ... have placed in the Order of Worship at that point, a statement that a part of the pastoral prayer was adapted from Wendy Wright, and a naming of the publication? Trouble is: that it is likely the Order of Worship had been printed before the Pastoral Prayer began to take shape. But it probably should have been done.

Reader Notes and Reflections

Reader Notes and Reflections

Reader Notes and Reflections

Reader Notes and Reflections

LET IT BE TO US ACCORDING TO YOUR WORD

Then Mary said, "Here am I, the servant of the Lord; let it be with me according to your word." Then the angel departed. (The "message" was complete.)

Are we waiting here this morning, God, in hushed expectation? Is it really like that? ... in hushed expectation, like children trying in vain to go to sleep on the night before the magic morning, really not knowing what to expect, but still waiting with that trusting expectation of the promise? Not really just this morning, but sensing every morning when the congregation gathers, to be such a moment? Wouldn't it be wonderful if we could be that way with you, God? Not really knowing, for the promised presents have never been seen unwrapped. And we know inside that if we could name it, even up to the level of our wildest dreams ... what you have for us would probably be so very much more than anything we could name or describe. But, then, God, could it be that the expectation in our hearts ... during our waiting in the night for the surprising unfoldings of the new-dawning day ... the _expectation_ is the greatest gift of all you have to give in such moments ... as we come to know that *always* you have more ... just waiting to be born in us and to us ... if we will but be as trusting as was Mary of your promise to implant and bring to life your very self within us?

Then, forgive us, God, when such expectations so often begin to dim during the night hours when we cannot see. Forgive us and help each one of us to discover the Mary-part of ourselves ... and allow that unexpectedly trusting part of ourselves to say, "Here I am, your servant; let it be to me according to your word." Here I am.

We need so much to trust (to stand upon) your promises to us. So, help us we pray, as a congregation awaiting a new day, to put away all doubts, hesitations, fears, misgivings, and to wait with all the hushed expectation of children unable to sleep for our excited wonder at what the morning may bring. Let it be to us according to your word (your promise). Thank you for what you have done, are doing, and will yet do with-and-through the expectant spirits we bring and present to you in these waiting together moments of each week.

We pray in the name and spirit of him whose birth in our midst simply must begin with such a Mary-response: "Here am I, the servant of the Lord; let it be to me according to your word." Amen

Reflections

I cannot honestly say that this is exactly the way the prayer came out that morning. As a matter of fact it most certainly came out more than one way. For it (as most of these) was used in two services. And I am certain that there was a further "unfolding," on the spot, of the theme which had emerged in the original preparation, as the Spirit continues to "blow as it will," to meet the unique situation. Surely other pastors will attest to this kind of "entering-in" of the Spirit when the presenter leaves enough chinks and cracks in the preparation for it to happen.

So, in this kind of process, the prayer may "get prayed" in several settings, hopefully with an evolution which makes it uniquely apropos for each occasion. Ideally the first "occasion" would be the actual prayer that is happening with the one individual who is preparing for the time of worship. Succeeding occasions would be each service where the prayer was prayed. But this comes up now because of trying to remember so long after the fact what kinds of evolution were happening during the prayer with the congregation. And I was left with a profound feeling of having been led into personal, prayer "of the moment" there in the early hours over the word-processor (or typewriter?) all of those years before. Now new experiences were welling up again in response to present personal needs and ... further growth. Wow!

Readers Reflections

EXCURSIS III
Maybe Narcissism Isn't All Bad

Alright ! ... this just might be the time to share something that has been nagging at me for several pages on this proofread of Lover's Dialog, getting it ready to print. It does seem to fit in the context of the "Reflections" of the page just completed.

I have already mentioned how the preparation, and then later review, of such things as pastoral prayers from the past, sometimes seems to make up at least a little bit for the sloppy and haphazard, and often times almost non-existent discipline of my own devotional life. It just struck me while proof reading the preceding prayer and reflections that such activities may not be (entirely, at least) the signs of a kind of self centered narcissism that delights in looking at itself by returning again to one's former products. I think maybe I had been beginning to fear this might be the case.

(Yes, it does feel good sometimes to pull up and read my own writings ... sometimes fondling them like King Midas running his hands through the piles of gold that he has horded away. And yes, there are sometimes feelings akin to the sensations of guilt that we sort-of insecure personalities are inclined to experience.)

But then, there was the insight that had also been growing: that I was also beginning to sense a growth of appreciation for some things which at one time had turned me cold. I speak of the grand old prayers and responses from the past which have been repeated over and over again through such liturgical tools as The Book of Common Prayer. Perhaps, as a "freed-up" member of the "free church" tradition, it was alright to have such feelings, *for a while* ... but might I not later "grow up" and begin to discover value in some of the things that I thought I had moved beyond. Couldn't this be a valid route to a next stage of maturity?

Well, anyway, what I am trying to express is the realization ... after some very moving occasions of worship where such "traditional prayerbook" materials had been sensitively used by others ... that such prayers, repeated from the tradition of the church, could be very deep and meaningful.

Then why, if re-reading my own material from the past seems to again nourish my soul, should I feel myself to be guilty of narcissism? Why shouldn't I appreciate being reminded again of what had been meaningful in the past? It's kind of like asking, "Why should I tell my wife that I love her? After all, I just told her that last week. Or was it last month?

So couldn't this be another argument for developing a discipline of reviewing and critiquing one's pastoral prayers, and other materials used in the development and direction of corporate worship? It just might have the potential of reminding and re-nourishing one's soul. What say you? kmborg1@aol.com

TAKING THE TIME TO BE A BABY

Can it be, O God, that it's OK to drag out this season of Advent the way we do because you really do come to us this way? Is there some-thing you are trying to communicate to our _hearts_ through this protracted Advent/ Christmas story, because you know that our _brains_ will never get it? ... a knowing somewhere down deep that you have the time, and will take whatever time it takes to really be born in our lives ...if we will just patiently expect and patiently await whatever planting of seeds, whatever fertilization and slow beginnings and gestation process it takes, whatever birth process, to be actually born into even the most common parts of our lives (as common as a barn out back), and then continue to grow slowly in our lives just like a child? ... so that it's OK to take time to be human ... to cry for mother's breast, to fly a kite and blow bubbles in the breezes, to laugh and to cry, to love and to fear and to mourn, to dance and to sing, to struggle and risk and make mistakes ... to die? That it's OK! God, do you draw us into this expectant waiting process to affirm our humanness, to somehow say, "It's all OK, and this is the way you really do come to know?"

Then, if this is so, help us, we pray, to affirm it along with you. Forgive us when we moan and complain of the commercialization; and help us to look for you in the process, just as you were entering in during the donkey-travel, and when there was no room at the inn. Help us to expect and be looking for your entering-in not only through our celebrations and our worship, but even through our illnesses and our dying. Not only through the shining moments of love and success, but also through those failures when we tried, but didn't quite make it. Not only when things just keep getting better and better, but also when things piddle out and end, and we must begin all over again.

Thank you, God, for taking time to become and to be a baby. We have needed to experience that ... and we guess we still do. You will help us to experience it again and again and again ... won't you?

In the spirit of the lover of our souls who seems willing to be, and continues to be, born in our lives and amidst us among the cattle in our outback barns ... because we are so busy with our censuses and resulting tax structures and getting rich producing and selling the materials we use to celebrate the birth ... that there is no room to be born anywhere else ...In the name of that one, we pray. Amen

Reflections

From penciled notes on the sheet I know there were specific pastoral concerns expressed during this time of pastoral prayer, but there is no way of knowing, a few years after, where they were shoe-horned in … very likely at different times in the first and the second services. Several of these pastoral concerns had obviously been relayed to me after the prayer had been prepared, and I can see now how some of them may have been used as illustrations of the human processes being described as metaphors of the incarnation. Isn't it this fitting and weaving together of the theological basis and the alternating joy and burden, that makes up the dynamics of the life of a congregation? Looked at this way, how serendipitous must be the seasons of Advent/Christmas, and Lent/Easter. What pastor can ever remember one of those seasons which wasn't "seasoned" by both tragedies and celebrations which surpassed any kinds of "canned" illustration/ metaphors which might have been dredged up from reading and from well-catalogued notes.

Yet how often does the congregation experience a great gulf between sermon, prayer, invitation to communion, etc., and the announcement of the member's experience of these Common Ventures of Life (as Elton Trueblood entitled one of his books). The experience of most any congregation at most any point in time is so rich and illustrative of what the faith is all about, but so often our worship services come across as "programs," when these rich experiences our Creator is continually providing us come to us as "announcements," instead of woven-in parts of the liturgy (defined, "the work of the laity"). Looking back, how I hope I was able to rise to the occasion. Maybe I should be glad that, after so long a time, there is no tape of the service to check it out … and my memory is so poor.

Reader Reflections

THE SEASONS OF OUR LIVES

Oh God—God of the seasons of our lives—as we gather this day when we are missing many of our number who are wise not to be here because it is simply too cold for them to be out of the warmth of their homes, help us to remember only a few months back and to look ahead but a few months to those times when our thinking, more appropriately could be, "Oh, I hope the air-conditioner is working well, or we will swelter for sure."

For in the procession of our lives we have come to look forward to seasons; seasons we can plan and depend upon, knowing that they will follow in order. But at the same time we know that each of them will be at least a little bit different. And so shall we as you walk with us in this wondrous, exciting journey through time and eternity.

So the season of winter has certainly come, as we knew it would. But we are a bit different, and some of our number no longer share this day in the journey with us, as we knew it would be. We worship together, as our parents-in-the-faith a hundred or so years ago were probably pretty certain we would be ... but the way we do it has evolved year-by-year, as they were probably pretty sure it would. They might be surprised to find us in such relative comfort instead of huddled around a little wood-burning stove, and would be simply bowled-over by the sound of our mighty organ (which no doubt some would have liked, and some would not).

And we still trust you to be in the process. We thank you for growth and the excitement of the new in the dependability of the season; for the promise of eternity even in the midst of change. You have known our need for both stability and change, and are with us through it all.

So, with an ever-growing trust, help us to continually place each of our lives, and the life of this congregation in your ever-dependable hands. For just a moment help us to see your arms around each of those for whom we specifically pray this day, meeting their needs with your eternal wisdom and strength _____
_____

Let each one picture those arms around them, personally as always, continuing to heal and to care ... as we commit ourselves personally and as a congregation into your loving, forgiving, care. In the name and the Spirit of the Christ, we pray. Amen

Reflections

Surely the congregation deserved more than this! These several years after, I can pretty well picture the process: After a drive through the bitter cold of a Michiana winter day and a walk from the relative warmth of the car to the blessed warmth of the building; probably figuring to lead without notes a prayer for the few who had braved the morning cold, then deciding there was time to put something down on paper as insurance against either drawing a blank, or rambling interminably. And this was what came out; sort of a free-association on the morning. Hopefully I was free enough not to have been tied too much to what was written, and let the Spirit enter in more in the pulpit than was the case in the preparation. But it was too long ago for me to remember, so I simply share here what was on the paper ... a rather weak attempt to open the door to invite the eternal into some reflections on the mundaneness of what was going on in time. Surely you have had times like this. Haven't you?

Reader Reflections

THAT MORNING ! ! !

Hear our praises, God, for the light of this fresh new morning! Hear our praises for the Good News of the wondrous light which the world had thought would never come. We understand the doubts and fears of the world, for they have been our doubts and fears, as well. We might have passed off the excitement of "The Day of Resurrection" (of which we have just sung) with little more than a "Ho-hum," if we had really expected it, but we have always been so much like the rest of them in their doubts and fears and lack of expectation. And it helps us to understand.

Whether we were watching through another "last supper," or trying agonizingly in prayer to give over our lives that Thursday night "in the garden," or carrying a Friday cross too heavy to bear ... whether experiencing our own seeming hopelessness and fear and dead-ends after our own hopes had been so high ... and it all came tumbling down ... we've feared and doubted (along with the rest of the world) that this was all there was, and any expectation of anything more was only kidding ourselves.

So we thank you so much for celebration mornings such as this, when at least it seems that those dreadful moments three days ago were not "all there is." We thank you so much and pray you will help us, now and forever more, to be able to hold ourselves open to the entering-in of your spirit ... so that, in the midst of those continual, pesky doubts, that spirit-of-truth within may keep whispering or shouting, "It is so! It is so! He has risen! And so shall you!" We know that we shall often doubt, and that is allowable, <u>but for now, it is so!</u>"

So that families , like the _____'s and _____ __'s. saying Goodbye just this week to their loved ones might say it trusting that there is yet more. So that those such as _____, awaiting your healing touch (however it may come), may wait trusting there is yet more. So that those rising to new life from the cleansing, burial waters of baptism this day may experience, beginning now, an eternal walk together with us and our Lord through the rest of our temporal days. So that, from now on, who ever comes in contact with those of us from "The Church on the Hill"* will so experience the risen Christ in our midst that their lives may never ever again be the same . . . .

So that we can celebrate 101 years with Clara Brown in the same joy and hope that we celebrate 1, or 10, or 20 ... or 39, without needing to say, "and holding." So that frowns of disapproval may begin to be replaced with smiles of acceptance and even love of our wondrous differences, and hugs of joy for our transformed humanness ... since we now know. Now, we know! He has risen! He is here! Now and forever!   Amen, Amen, Amen!

* As this building is known by the neighborhood, because of it's distinctive, highly visible location

Reflections

I simply liked this one, and realize that sometimes I get so caught up in my own stuff that it is utterly impossible to reflect on it objectively. So I'll just leave it alone. You do the reflecting … and don't be embarrassed if you feel I would be embarrassed by your reflections.

Reader Reflections

FREED FROM FEAR, RAISED UP AND SENT OUT

Finally, finally, O God, we begin to stir again from the bleak winter of our lives, as the warm breath of Spring seduces us to believe that maybe there really will always be rebirth and new life; and that maybe it really does come, not from any renewed vigor, or gritted-teeth determination on our part to scratch our living from the earth ... but, instead, as that ever-surprising-new-each-time <u>gift</u>. So now we look back at our most recent dryness and say, "Come from the 4 winds, O breath, and breathe into our deadnesses that we may live!"... and that there may be continual Easter Joy, and Laughter, and Light ... rising up out of the dry-dead-bones-ache and solemnity of Lent. O Breather of life-from-the-4-winds, we pray that, in spite of our hard-ness of heart, you will continue to breath your perennial Spring Breath into the faith that we share together ... so that one such as_____, hovering between death and life may simply know-within that nothing in all creation can separate us from your love, and his family may be free to let go, and go out in (eventual) joy ... that one such as _____ may so submit and open her life, that medicines and therapies and immune systems may join together in the healing dance for which they are intended (however that healing may come) ... that we may all "walk with" Rick Bell as he trustingly learns, again and again, to walk amongst us* ... and that _____ _____ _____ may know across the distance, that we walk with her in caring and prayer... and that those who carry with them the contagious joy of youth may not give up on the rest of us, and the sometimes dryness of our bones. And at the same time that we become more and more willing to be infected with what they hold out to us. O Giver of Life and Breath, many of us here have experienced your touch upon our lives in such powerful (sometimes quietly powerful) ways that we are very careful who we tell, for fear they will laugh and tell us it was only an accidental, emotion, and doubt the stability of our minds. Won't you free us from such fears? ... so that we may begin, more freely each day, to share with the great congregation the glad news of our deliverance from the dry bones of a faithless life! We hunger so for the warm infilling of your Easter presence, but we live lives of so much timidity and fear. So our prayer today is that you continue to send out those of us who can and will proclaim the breathing of life into the dryness of our bones and raise us up with the Christ, in whose name we pray. Amen.

*after yet another surgical whittling away of his feet, from the ravages of diabetes.

Reflections

Woops! Have I just cast a jaundiced eye upon the traditional celebrations of the season of Lent in the liturgical calendar? It was certainly not intended, but it could be read to sound that way. I really do believe that when individuals and congregations try genuinely and sincerely to observe the season of Lent it serves its purpose: expressing the realization that genuine new life so often grows out of the desert-bleak-ness situations of our lives. It makes the all-out celebration of Easter that much more joyful for the contrast. And it seems to make sense to point up and to offer up in prayer the reality of that contrast. But, still, I can see how sensitively such things must be worded, lest they alienate those who would not understand. Apparently I just wasn't thinking of that when this was put together, and I know I need to become more sensitive to such possibilities.

Reader Reflections

HAVE YOU NOT KNOWN ? ?

Following the reading of Isaiah 40:21-31

Now that the question has been raised, O God, we may have to admit that probably we have not known ... who you are. Oh, we may have heard about you, but we have not understood from the foundations of the earth, as the scripture asks us. So we pray now for open eyes, here in this place, to at least begin to see and to understand; maybe eventually to begin to know you ... you who slip into our everyday lives ... and renew our strength ... and cause us to mount up as eagles, and not be overcome by the weariness of a world literally starving to know ... they know not what. When, really, the hunger is for you.

Could it be possible, O God, that we are, right now, in the place of all places to begin to come to some kind of working knowledge of how you reach out with power to the faint and strength to the powerless (such as we)? We look around us and we see here a family of those who have chosen to reach out together for a knowledge of you. We want to "hold together" in Christ, according to the promise. But there are vacant places today. Helen Barnes is not among us. Hear our prayer ... together ... for Helen as she leaves the hospital again to the next phase of her life. As she waits upon you, may she renew her strength and mount up with wings like an eagle, and may our prayer together-for-her enter into it as she discovers yet more dimensions of your love for her ...your quiet power-in-the-midst of weakness. As _____ _____ and _____ walk with you through their times of illness and weakness, use us, we pray, as agents of the knowledge of you ... you who give power to the faint and strengthen the powerless ... sometimes, maybe with the best power of all: the power simply to let go and rest back in those parental arms in the knowledge that they will never let go. What power that may take in the midst of a culture that worships so many lesser kinds of "power." May this family of faith really "hold together" in Christ and discover in the "holding together" that quiet lifting up like soaring eagle wings, not even moving, but borne up by the unseen flow of your spirit through it all. We pray this kind of peace for _____and _____ .

Thank you, God, for the peace that comes with trust that you really are intimately involved with all you have created and are creating. Thank you for calling us into this part of the Body of Christ, through which you reach out to us and to the world whenever we will allow you to be the heart of our life together. Forgive us when we keep missing the point and forget the privilege of participating in your continuing creation by simply "being-here-together" for one another and for the world. We really want to "hear" and to "know" you. We hunger and thirst for such hearing and knowing. And if knowing one another in the light of your love is where this may begin, then please, God, open the eyes of our hearts. Our prayers may not always be in the spirit of Jesus, the Christ, but we want them to be. So help us, we pray, to see, to trust, and, finally, to know … in that Spirit … in that Name.   Amen

Reflections

Reflecting on this I find myself asking why more pastoral prayers are not deliberately related to specific readings of scripture? How connecting to the source of it all, this can be. Could it be that such a question relates back to that constantly recurring fear that the congregation might feel that the prayer had been "used" as a way of slipping in one more sermon? But why not "learning through prayer?" Is not all valid prayer an expression of learning, or struggling to learn of … to know, as we have been saying here … the One to whom we pray? Is it not prayer in the deepest sense when we learn more deeply the heart of the One to whom we pray? In beginning to reproduce this prayer from its original notes I had to leave the word processor and bring up my computer Bible concordance to remind myself in which chapter of Isaiah these so-familiar words were found. How I am wishing, now, that all those foundational years had been more filled with such minute-by-minute inflowing of this nurturing resource.   I wonder how many others of my generation were as pleased as I when Bibles began to be available which could be carried in inside pockets so we could have them along in case of need, yet would not be categorized with those who we judged to be "pretentious" as they carried their huge black Bibles with them wherever they went. Right now, as I reflect, my prayer is "God, forgive me for the judgementalism that may have sometimes insulated me from those who might have been part of the treasure you were holding out for me to take.

Reader Responses

MAGNIFY AND EXALT YOUR NAME TOGETHER

Following the reading of Psalm 34:1-3

O God, we really do want to bless you at all times; we want your praise to continually be in our mouths to magnify you and exalt your name together … we really do. But then someone really offends us, and we simply turn our backs and dig in our heels and refuse to acknowledge and accept them, no matter how sorry and contrite; we become guardians against, rather than ambassadors of reconciliation, and it never dawns upon us that, in this, we are mocking (rather than blessing and praising) you; we are diminishing your presence in our lives and the world around, rather than magnifying and exalting your name together.

Forgive us, O God, as you run down the road to greet a returning son or daughter, and we turn our backs and break your heart … the very heart that is the pulsing, throbbing center of all there is. Forgive us when we will upon ourselves sickness of body and heart and soul, as individuals or as a congregation, while you are trying to woo us into oneness and wholeness … into health, contagious health. Forgive us!

And then, O God, help us to begin to accept that forgiveness, to make it a part of who we basically are, so that you may, indeed be able to help us to open our hearts, to unclench our fists and reach out, to unclog our ears and clear our eyes … to see and take hold of … and affirm … the amazing opportunities into which you seem to be trying to lead us through these exciting days and weeks and years of transition and growth and adventure with you. Help us to let go of the coldness of our stubbornness and skepticism and fears, and to allow you to draw us into the warmth of your healing love, so that we may then be channels of that love to those of our number whom we bring before you this day. _____and_____.

We pray that we, together here today, may be one of the channels of love to our own community. Why, we even have the audacity to pray for the belief that our struggling-towards-faithfulness-lives might some how become channels of love to the world … so much of that world up to now starving in separateness. We acknowledge your invitation during the remainder of our worship to partake of that love feast, which is always the climax of our worship, and which can never be fully celebrated alone. Help us, we pray, to accept the invitation, and pray our prayers in the name and the Spirit of Jesus, the Christ, who yearns for us all to be a loving responsive part of all that is. Amen

Response

Once again I wish I could better remember what had been going on at the time of this prayer. If I were reading it cold as someone else's prayer I would be suspicious that the person doing it was using prayer to subtly sneak in a little lecture on forgiveness to an audience which was captive to the prayer. I honestly don't think I was doing anything that blatant, but know I am not above being captive to unconscious impulses which I probably wouldn't acknowledge if confronted.

But that brings up a question with which I must begin to deal: Assuming I were in a congregational setting where there was an inordinate amount of judgment, unforgiveness and unwillingness to consent to moves toward reconciliation. Would not my own personal prayer life be sometimes dominated by such concerns? Would I not want to subtly draw the congregation more and more towards a prayerful consideration of such concerns? Wouldn't it be natural to include this sort of thing in the Pastoral Prayer, and wouldn't those who shared my concerns be short-changed if it were never included in the Sunday morning liturgy? But wouldn't the congregation feel that I was, maybe, beating them over the head with it from a privileged position? How could I know whether I was doing this in a healthy way or a sneaky way? Or am I making a non-issue into an issue? I am not sure, and am glad this prayer from the past came up; for it tells me I still have so much to learn.

Reader Response

LEANING INTO A SENSE OF BELONGING

O God, as we gather this morning to celebrate the final days of the summer-that-never-happened, it is with a special sense of the way in which you, and you alone, seem able to bind everything together so that every part and every one shares in the destiny of every other part and every other one. Forgive us where we refuse to see this happening and insist upon remaining orphans where you have intended us to be family ... where we persist in building walls and boundaries when you long to see us throwing up bridges across the painful chasms yawning between us.

Today as we celebrate work and our vocations, the tasks you have called upon each of us to do, we pray for a vision of the way my task interweaves with my neighbor's task, and our tasks interweave the tasks of those around us so that we become servants of one-another. Help us to see how important we are to each other as we affirm and commit to one-another in our times of wedding, and graduation and promotion, and for the same reasons lean upon and grieve with one another in our times of funeral and loss to the great, irresistible tides of nature ... in our homes, our congregation, our land, our world, into the farthest reaches of the unfathomable mystery which you have given us as our own "Garden of Eden," to enhance or despoil as we choose. What a wonderful and risky gift you have given us in our freedom!

Especially today, as many of us grasp at the last chance of the season to enjoy a bit of holiday recreation, we pray a sense of your presence, restraining us from working so hard at our play that it never really becomes play, so that we never really see and connect with one another in the process ... as you restrain us from working at play at the same time that you pour out on us the wonderful freedom to revel in your creation amongst the sisters and brothers and aunts and uncles and cousins and cherished neighbors of this both local and global village.

Only you can free us to relax and lean into it with a sense of belonging and destiny. Only you can help us to see one-another as your gifts to one-another. *Only you.* In whose name and whose spirit we pray.

Amen

Reflections

Doing these reflections continues to remind me how much I (and I am certain most everyone) lean on little pet expressions, such as "being orphans when God had intended us to be family." This is sort of a come-uppance to one who tends to be impatient with the "jargon" of "other" parts of the family of faith. How did I say it?: "... so 'jargony' that, if you move in the same circles, you may be able to finish the sentence before the leader of the prayer gets there." So, if it's me it is "little pet expressions;" if it is "them," it is "jargony." Ouch! But, on the other hand, we are often known by and sometimes loved for those expressions which are characteristic of us and may communicate what we want to say. How could I possibly expect to present a year's prayers and have no such repeats? Jesus apparently did it without it sounding like a "party line;" the Apostle Paul, also. I guess we walk a tight-rope most of the time, and had best remember that it really is a tight-rope, and not forget to carry our balancing rod. Then the appropriate response is probably to be able to identify and to know how to use your own balancing rod. I wonder if these kinds of reflections are such an "appropriate response?"

Readers Reflections

FOR THE LONG VIEW

Eternal God; God of our yesterdays, our todays and our tomorrows; God who puts together our yesterdays, our todays and our tomorrows ... who puts them together so that they fit ... and each gives meaning to the other ... we come together on this day of transition ... from yesterday through today and into tomorrow ... with a profound sense of your presence, filling us, surrounding us, pointing us in directions we may not have foreseen, but directions which are unfolding and will, indeed, take us somewhere. Well, maybe what I have just said isn't entirely true. Forgive us if it isn't always with such a profound sense of your presence that we come. (For most of us, at least some of the time.) If sometimes there may be periods of merely "going through the motions" in the hope that again, eventually, it will feel right, and the trust will return. It's all right if we come ... some-times ... like that, isn't it? Forgive us our lack of trust that you really do have the whole world in your hands, when the directions do not seem to be the ones we would have chosen; and remind us who is at the helm, and that we really are "all in the same boat"... not just this congregation, not just this denomination, not just we mainliners, not even just the Christian faith, but all who truly seek you from other traditions ... all of us in the same boat.

So it is the long view for which we pray today. On this week-end when we celebrate our nationhood, help us to begin day-by-day to celebrate the beauty, not only of our nation, but of our species ... to celebrate the ties of our common humanity ... to glory in our responsibilities to all of life upon this planet earth,to long for bridges to span our differences, and for the grit to continue dismantling the many walls which have been so long a-building amidst the fear and distrust of those of us who have not been able to hear the call and follow the lead of the One who you have raised up for us to come to know and follow. (And we know that sometimes the fear and distrust is located right in our own hearts.)

Oh, we realize that our praying sounds so lofty and pretentious some-times, so now let us come down to earth, as we simply ask that you be with us whether we "feel" it or not. Help us to know that it is alright ... that you really do honor it when those of us who do not right now "feel" it, still go through the motions (like husband and wife who continue to kiss, though little is felt, in trust that continuing in loving ways may eventually result in the return of the sense of love, which means so much). We don't always really trust the directions in which you take us. We confess that. But we do want to ... so hear our prayers and help us to trust ... as we continue to learn from Jesus, the Christ, in whose name and spirit we pray. Amen

Reflections

Whew! What a mixing of metaphors. But I like that; I cannot make sense of my life without reference to the sometimes jumbled metaphors which help me to see the unfolding meaning in it … likening those things which are still mysteries to other things I have begun to understand. And my contention has always been that prayers which fit the canons of "good writing and composition" might be nice, but still lack the "juice of life" that connects our humanness to the hopes and intentions (and yearnings?) of a Bodacious, Lover/God. If the "only in His-name-Christian-hardliners" were looking for evidence to nail me they certainly have found it here. I would hope that such misunderstandings could sometimes be clarified through dialog about what those words mean, but seldom do such questionings become face-to-face. So my decision has been to stick my neck out and express what has been growing in my heart. And absorb whatever may ensue.

Whatever my intention in confessing that some of us may not "feel" what we are trying to pray; I recognize that it will be understood by some as a "projection" of myself onto the "we" which refers to the congregation itself. So be it! How unexpected it was once when the example: "like husband and wife who continue to kiss, though little is felt" was used in congregational prayer, and was later returned to me by a couple who said they had picked up on it and it may have saved their marriage. So this could be seen as blatantly aimed at specific situations. I don't remember that it was here, but guess the rightness or wrongness of such aiming would be up for grabs. In the context of prayer such a hint might be picked up in a more dynamic way than in therapy. And who knows what The Spirit might have had in mind in the dialog as this one was prayed at the word-processor before it was ever prayed from the pulpit?

Reader Reflections

EXCURSIS IV
Worship as Dance

More middle of the night nagging … by what … or by Whom?:

Somehow I have been awakened by a question picking away at me in the wee hours of the night; now up and sitting at my desk. Feels like an invitation into some kind of dialog. But invitation by whom?; On what subject? For some reason my eye flits up to the book-shelf and lands on a thin, green book that someone gave me for Christmas a few years ago, and which I haven't done more than leaf through. My hand reaches up and pulls it down. Hmmm: C.S. Lewis – on – **JOY**[5] … little selected excerpts compiled by Lesley Walmsley from Lewis's writings. Check the table of contents: There is a two pager, excerpted from MERE CHRISTIANITY, entitled here, "A Kind of Dance:"

"In Christianity God is not a static thing – not even a person – but a dynamic, pulsing activity, a life, almost a kind of drama. Almost, if you will not think me irreverent, a kind of dance. The union between Father and Son is such a live concrete thing that this union itself is also a Person … What grows out of the joint life of the Father and Son is a real Person, is in fact the Third of the three Persons who are God …This third Person is called the Holy Ghost or the 'spirit' of God. (We've used the term 'the Presence.')

"And now, what does it all matter? It matters more than anything else in the world. The whole dance, or drama, or pattern of this Three Personal life is to be played out in each one of us: or (putting it the other way round) each one of us has got to enter that pattern, take his/her place in the dance. There is no other way to the happiness for which we are all made. Good things as well as bad, you know, are caught by a kind of infection. If you want to get warm you must stand near to the fire; if you want to be wet you must get into the water. If you want joy, power, peace, eternal life, you must get close to, or even into, the thing that has them. They are not a sort of prize which God could, if He chose, just hand out to anyone. They are a great fountain of energy and beauty spurting up at the very center of reality. If you are close to it, the spray will wet you; if you are not, you will remain dry. Once a (person) is united to God, how could (that person) not live for ever?"[1]

Is that what we have been talking about in these pages? Is it that if you want to get wet you must stand close, as opposed to standing (or sitting) there watching someone else trying to stand close? Is it that you must be taking part in the dance; swaying together in alternation between stepping ahead

---

[5] C.S. Lewis – on – **Joy,** Thomas Nelson Publishers, Nashville, 1998, *Compiled by Lesley Walmsley,* Pp 30-31.

and stepping back in sinuous synchrony with another? ... <u>The</u> Dance. What is such a dance? ... but Dialog.

But so many have honestly thought of attending congregational worship as a kind of spectator sport, or as a promotional, educational experience, directed by professional Masters of Ceremony. What a basic difference!

Is that why, when the congregation where I was visiting had joined in the processional hymn, singing those soaring words by van Dyke to a heart-stirring Beethoven 9th Symphony melody:

"Joyful, joyful, we adore thee, God of Glory, God of love;
hearts unfold like flowers before thee, op'ning to the
sun above.
Melt the clouds of sin and sadness, drive our fear and doubt
away; Giver of immortal gladness, fill us with the light of day."

(--I can swing and sway to that ...
but I can't do it alone ...
all of creation needs to join in ...
spontaneously ...
beginning with those around me ...
as music, and the spoken word ...
and the untranslatable bubbling of the heart ...
and the praise of the soul ...
all interwine in the dance ...)

but when that magnificent "invitation to worship" song was done, but vibrating silently there in the air, someone ambled over to the lectern and ... instead of simply allowing a moment of pregnant silence, and then continuing an unbroken morning liturgy by beginning the well-chosen responsive words printed in the Order of Worship ... said, "Good morning, isn't it a beautiful day?

"Would you please take your Order of Worship and read with me the Morning Litany" ...

I felt as if someone had stuck a pin in my balloon and I deflated with it into a squishy inert blob. So, from that moment on, I had to lecture myself about such an egotistical judgementalism as I had apparently been caught up in, and to really concentrate on entering in ... lest the whole affair should descend, for me, from the soaring, contagious worship begun by the singing together of that hymn, to become, from then on, the program-theme of the morning, announced and directed by one or more MC's from the Chancel.

126

Why had I actually become *ANGRY;* angry enough to ruin the whole experience of worship for me? Who did I think I was?! I was being like an ungrateful guest, sneering at the food placed on the table.

Standing Among the Wallflowers

Looking back right now ... here in the wee hours of the morning ... I can see it all, and hang my head for being so judgmental. But the sensation was one of having been invited to the *dance*, and all of a sudden being let down, for here I was surrounded by "wallflowers" ... by a roomful of people supposedly dedicated to the dance ...yet dampening the festivity by each one standing around on the periphery as an individual, separated from the others and from the One who was calling them into the dance. And I could remember, so well, Bruce Larson's wonderful little book of a generation ago, about the contagious dynamic of the Christian faith, entitled, "ASK ME TO DANCE."

Perhaps many of us had never felt really asked into the dance.

Forgive me, God! But, where do we go from here?

AFTER-WORD

In my current state of retirement, each week I lift up my eyes and note that the chancel of the building where I worship is dominated by an immense stained-glass interpretation of the Old Testament theme of "streams in the desert." How appropriate! ... here in this "desert wilderness-garden" of Las Vegas! (where, because two daughters and their families have made this their home, it could comfortably be chosen by Mary and me as our winter haven).

Several years ago I stumbled across an eye-opening way of looking at the really Good News (Gospel) of the Christian Faith. It would begin with the question: "What was the '*beginning*' of the Good News?" Only rarely could anyone come up with a quick, concise answer ... until they would be referred to the very *first* paragraph of the *earliest* written (Gospel) account of the remembered life of Jesus Christ:

> *The beginning of the good news of Jesus Christ, the Son of God ... the voice of one crying out in the wil-derness.* Mark 1:1-3

Oh! ...

...It begins as a voice, *crying out ... in the wilderness!?*

Really??

Well ...really ... isn't that often the way it is?: Life, created to be lived out in a veritable garden of delight, has somehow come down to being grubbed out in a desert wilderness. Gradually the silent, inner desert wilderness begins to foster **dialog**, with the *mystery* of it all; and so often the dialog begins to take the form of an inner conversation with a sort-of-remembered, sort-of-just-being-discovered, always-mysterious, **Presence** ...

... often beginning with the cry, "Why me? ! !"

Eventually there may be a response:

"I know, I know. I, your creator, hear you ... really hear you. I've been where you are. ("Why have you forsaken me?'; remember?) So I know ... and I've been *yearning* for you ...waiting here in this familiar desert wilderness. Here, know that I am listening. Perhaps *here* we may each be able to speak and to be heard, all in the same moment ... as lovers do." It's always been an invitation to a date: "Go with me to the Dance. We'll come to know one-another in the shared following and leading of the Dance."

The Desert and the Oasis

Though I loved my role as Director of Pastoral Care at a community hospital in the Midwest it was very difficult to feel adequate to the task. How could one "practice what he preached" about inner peace while scurrying from one demand to another? At one point I began giving myself permission once or twice a day to close my office door, forward the phone, and spend 15 or 20 minutes away from it all. One of the most helpful ways to do this was to sit quietly and walk myself through a kind of guided imagery.

For several days at one period I chose to take seriously the wildernesses of my own life by picturing myself struggling through the silent bleakness of a desert, sighting an oasis off in the distance, and walking into it. Each day I would get further into the oasis, until one day I was surprised to hear the tinkling sound of running water. Following the sound I found myself right in the center of the oasis, where a spring of water was bubbling up out of the top of a little hillock and running into a quiet pool down below. It was so satisfying, each day, to sit down in the grass and just enjoy the sight and the sound, assuming that it would always be there for me. My Oasis in the desert.

But one day something strange about that scene began to catch my attention. Though the bubbling flow of water was constant, the little pool at the base of the hillock never got any larger; so I went over to take a closer look. There it began to make sense. Tiny rivulets of water were flowing off through the grass in all directions, and some-thing "clicked" in my head (heart?). That little spring at the center was gradually watering the desert. No, the desert was so vast that it would likely never be totally green, but as long as I took time out to let this vision become a part of my reality I was assured that the desert would always be at least a little bit smaller, and the oasis a little bit larger.

Of course the above experience and the understanding of it was the result of an inner dialog, which expanded over several days. Most people would say, "Down, boy, it was just your imagination." OK, so be it. But, still, it had a life of its own like a dialog. So who was the initiator? I felt loved and I loved back. And the feeling loved and the loving back couldn't be separated; it was a living dialog, all in the same instant.

An Eternal Cycle ?

Wouldn't it be nice if I could say, "Ever since then I have known that kind of inner peace." But you would know I was lying.

On the other hand, if I were to say something like: "Oh yes, finally I'm beginning to see that the story of my life has become an eternal cycle: Finding myself in the desert wilderness again; discovering once more the oasis there which speaks to me and re-introduces me to the quiet, continually flowing peace of the eternal heart there at the center". . . .

If I were to put it that way, do you suppose it might be possible for you, also, to recognize a similar recurring cycle in your own experience?

And if that were the case, wouldn't it almost seem that *both* parts of the experience ... both the dry wilderness and the flowing, nourishing stream at the heart ... are about equally essential to *anyone* who aspires to live as a loving and creative part of such a struggling human family as this world has come to be?

Even if something so drastic
as death
followed by the exploding surprise
of resurrection
should be the ultimate
defining illustration

Listening to the Arroyo

A few years ago I found myself living right on the edge of one of the "Green-Way" parks which snake their way amongst some of the residential areas of Las Vegas. This soon became the site of my 3 ½ mile daily aerobic walks. Only gradually did I began to realize that this was really a converted "arroyo"… an ancient, dry gully river bed, which once or twice during the year might come to life and carry the local rains and snow-melt from the surrounding mountains down the valley into Lake Mead, at the foot of Boulder Dam. It seemed a natural setting for the Parks Department to nudge into shape for use by its citizenry.

It took a few seasons for me to realize I was looking forward to these daily sessions for more than just their exercise value. What I began to realize was that the arroyo was … *by its very nature* … speaking to me at a rather deep inner level; and I began sometimes coming back from these "walks" and writing down a page of such observations (as of this writing numbering just under 40 pages). Of course there was the message which the world of nature promises to speak to most anyone who will really look and listen; but the real *essence of the arroyo* began to make itself known through the mingling of the dry-desert-ness of the central stream bed with the lovely greenness of the foliage along the dry banks, which was nourished and watered by the occasional natural inundations spilling over its banks, and the trickles of targeted watering provided by the Department of Parks. So now, besides the polar opposites--of night and day, war and peace, female and male, spirit and matter, hot and cold, love and hate, positive and negative--the new category of dry and moist (brown and green) began to impinge upon my vision … a new sense of beauty and meaning seen when these two "poles" were allowed and encouraged to put the interaction between such polar opposites into a new focus.

Personally, I began to see that the term "bi-polar" might describe not only a disease listed in health care diagnostic manuals; but that most *everyone* is at least a bit "bi-polar" in their orientation to reality. And sometimes the ability to accept and love these traits of polarity in myself and in others may be the most redeeming trait of all.

Then, share with me, will you, two pages from the "**ARROYO**" manuscript; pages written under the heading of "Soul."

SOUL

Starting down the arroyo on this particular day something begins picking at the gut, that feels strangely old and basic; a feeling of, I've been here before;

long ago. It's like: this is a part of me ... a part of my heritage. Hmm ... better ponder this.

Somehow today the landscape had come alive. I could almost see men chasing and dodging one another, peering out from behind the rocks and firing at one-another with rifles and six-shooters, bullets ricocheting off the rocks. Almost, I could hear in my head exciting back-ground music as an accompaniment to the scenario..

Ah, there was the clue. And it said so much about the appeal of the arroyo for those of us who accept and use this gift of the municipality to its people. Who in this country ... at least any who are over 50 years of age ... has not at one time or another felt defined as a citizen of a land with a rugged western frontier ... sort of an eternal growing edge? We have been brought up on "horse operas" where the "range" was not only "home," but where life was defined by the struggles between the white-hats and the black hats. That's who we are. Such feelings have been fed by an abundance of Zane Grey type literature. Whether or not we have ever been west of the Mississippi, still we have seen so many movies filmed in landscapes just like this, that it has tunneled into our brains, and homesteaded a claim there.

Who among us has not heard parts of a Dvorak symphony, and maybe didn't know the music by name, but, hearing it, found pictures forming up in the brain, of wagon trains or horseback riders moving across the magnificent mountain backgrounds of the "western frontier?" Here a 19th century European composer had been so enthralled by the magnificence of the "New World" that his symphonic expression of that "New World" has been used as background music to define it for those of us who now populate it, and been the inspiration of other screen music composers,. until our souls resonate to the sound with mental pictures of "spacious skies and purple mountain majesties."

And *right here !* ... a block or so from my front door ... I can unlock and step through a steel gate daily and track a typical dry mountain stream (arroyo) from right out of that heritage, and let my mind wander until it may be captured by unexpected visions of the soul of the land I love through strength and weakness. I would swear I heard the voice of my soul say, one day, "Thanks, I needed that. And I hadn't even been certain I *had* one.

Was one ?

SOUL BUILDING

But then, the response of my wife, Mary, to the above began to open up a whole new vista of the arroyo. Her question was, didn't the Dvorak symphony point more to the grandeur of the mountains and the "big sky" country than to the little ole dry arroyo?

133

Looking around the day after, I had to agree that she was right: that part of the majestic mountain view of the arroyo picked up by the symphony was expressive of the grandeur of the West. And I am certainly tuned to the uplift urged on by such a combination of a beautiful land and sky and its background music.

But that morning another side to such a view begin to trickle in. You've got to know that for every breathtaking scene interpreted by the heart and mind, and musical scores of inspired human beings, there are dozens of little dry gullies which carry off the drainage of the mountains, and often this is where the people live ... and love ... and sometimes duke it out for their "rights," ... and die. The one is dove-tailed into the other, and the scenes are never complete until you turn your gaze down from the peaks to experience the scratching out of a living during seasons of drought.

The people in the gullies gotta look up, and the people on the mountains gotta look down, if _either_ is to experience a kind of reality that may not be fair, but that nevertheless offers a setting for the realization and growth of "soul." The symphony composer must have sensed that and reflected it. For laced in amongst the soaring, eye uplifting expressions of awe-inspiring beauty, you will find other sensitive renditions drawing the ear up next to the hurting, but ever-hopefulness of the slave, or the down-and-outer cowpoke, who might never find a home more grand than the gully. So the soaring chords may move swiftly back down to the andante theme, which would later be adapted to the "goin' home, goin' home," expression of one who's only remaining hope must be some better hereafter. (My father used to be asked to sing at funerals the same melody with words like: "Down de road; down de road; on my way to home. Tired and blue; weary, too; never more to roam.") And the composer has these seemingly opposite themes all tangled up with one another so that they reach inside you and speak what words alone could never say.

Going up and down the arroyo, one's eyes may glory in the surrounding, indomitable mountains, and then swing back down to where an active imagination could paint in a run-down, makeshift cabin on the small patch of grass with a couple of rough tomb-stones over there alongside that stream which seems never to flow. And who is to say which vista is the most likely to bequeath the treasure of "soul" to those who have passed this way? My guess is that it is the weaving together ... like hidden gullies, realistically clinging to the stake they have wrestled out from the mountain ... that inspires the living background melodies; and shapes the soul.

Shouldn't our lives and our prayers ... especially our prayers in a setting of worship together ... be occasions where the eternal weaving together of the majestic mountains and the dry gullies of each of our lives become dominant parts of the creative process of loving, living dialog between church, world, and God? I *think* that is what I believe. How about *you*?

Amen

About the Author
J. Kent Borgaard

The early "nudgings" began to take form during summer youth conferences at Sylvandale at the foot of the Big Thompson Canyon, down stream from Estes Park in Colorado. With W W II always running in the back ground, the nudgings seemed to be pointing to a vision involving some kind of healing ministry. But times were lean and the US Navy stepped in to provide 4 years of Education at the University of Utah, resulting in a BA degree in Sociology, and then 3 very formative years of active duty as an officer on aircraft carriers with Task Force 77 in the Pacific during the Korean conflict. Salt Lake City had also been the source of Mary; wife, lover, and creative, life-time companion.

The navy experience was followed by a brief time in the business world, before that old hankering began to return, and he and Mary, and their two young daughters packed all their worldly goods in a U-Haul trailer and headed from Spokane, WA to the Drake University Divinity School in, Des Moines, IA, for his M Div. Degree. There were yet to be two sons, rounding out the family.

After 24 years as a pastoral minister in the midwest, with brief collateral duties as Chaplain in the Navy Reserve, and Intermittent Chaplain at the Veterans Hospital in Des Moines, IA, Kent became Director of Pastoral Care at a 340 bed General Hospital in Elkhart, IN, and the evolution continued, leading him into another role as Pastoral Services Coordinator at Oaklawn, a major Psychiatric and Community Mental Health Complex in north central Indiana. He feels peculiarly blessed to have been able to experience such a variety of Pastoral Care roles during a most satisfying career.

Printed in the United States
80908LV00005B/96